COPING WITH LOSS
FOR PARENTS

Pat Elliot

Piccadilly Press • London

Designed by Zena Flax
Printed and bound by WBC, Bridgend
for the publishers Piccadilly Press Ltd.,
5 Castle Road, London NW1 8PR

A catalogue record for this book is available from
the British Library

ISBN: 1 85340 453 5

Other books in the How To Help Your Child series:
SPELLING FOR PARENTS
GRAMMAR FOR PARENTS
READING FOR PARENTS
MATHS FOR PARENTS
INFORMATION TECHNOLOGY FOR PARENTS
WRITING FOR PARENTS
CHILD SAFETY FOR PARENTS
OVERCOMING BULLYING FOR PARENTS

Cover design by Paul Cooper

COPING WITH LOSS
FOR PARENTS

To all those who are there to support
grieving children

Pat Elliot has worked for over ten years as
a counsellor and trainer, previously having been a
schoolteacher and tutor in Adult Education. Whilst
teaching she completed further qualifications in
group facilitation and an Advanced Diploma in
Counselling and Psychotherapy. Since then her
experience has included working as a counsellor in
middle school, high school and in higher education,
and in running a bereavement service. Over the years
she has led many parenting groups, and trained
professionals and volunteers both in counselling skills
and bereavement issues. At present she lives in
Wimbledon with her husband, son and two cats,
writes poetry, and divides her professional time
between a general psychotherapy practice in
Wimbledon, running workshops and courses for
schools and parents focussing on ways of supporting
bereaved children, and developing support for
women bereaved in childhood.

CONTENTS

INTRODUCTION

This book is written for you – parents or other adults, carers of children. It is written from my belief that children who suffer major losses need, and deserve, a high level of support. For this to be available, you need to know how best to be of help. It is my aim to pass on what I have learned about the way children grieve, and to suggest practical ways in which you can support your child.

Losses, major changes or bereavements happen to all of us. Death itself is the one certainty in life. So this book is not just for those parents whose children have suffered loss, but for all parents, to help prepare your children for future loss, so that when the time comes, they can cope more easily. You can prepare your child, whatever his/her age, to deal with loss just as you teach him or her about every other facet of life.

Some of what I write may be familiar – but some of the newer perspectives can be useful. Not all the practical ideas will work for you or for your child. We are each different and different things work for individual people, although there are patterns of similarities. These ideas are suggestions, not prescriptions. The important thing is to understand the processes of grieving and to have a number of helping strategies to try, so that you can find the ones that work for you and your child.

I have tried to make the book user-friendly, to work

either as a 'read-through' or as a 'reference'. If you are currently grieving, for instance, I suggest you turn directly to Chapters One and Five, for practical ideas on helping your child (although I do also mention these ideas briefly elsewhere), and to the Appendices which have suggestions for further support.

The examples given come from over twenty-nine years of working with children (as a teacher, counsellor and therapist in a variety of settings), and also from my work with adults, many of whom have spoken of the effects of childhood bereavement. No example represents an individual child or young person, so that identities are protected.

My sincere thanks to all those people – clients, colleagues, friends and family – who have helped me in this work and to put this book together. I hope that it will be of use to parents and hence to children whose needs in the areas of loss, change and bereavement have not always been easily recognised.

For the theoretical models of loss and grief, I have drawn in particular on the ideas of John Bowlby, Colin Murray-Parkes and William Worden, and the developmental models of Piaget and Erikson. I am also indebted to other colleagues in the field for sharing practical ideas. It is difficult to say where many of these originated.

Chapter One
BEREAVEMENT, LOSS AND CHANGE AND HOW CHILDREN MAY BE AFFECTED

HOW ARE BEREAVEMENT, LOSS AND CHANGE CONNECTED?

Loss is everywhere in life – from the time at birth when we leave the warm comfort of the womb, changing this for the intermittent security of our mother's arms, to the time when, becoming elderly, we may lose hearing, physical strength and memory. Loss occurs when we move house, when we end a friendship or relationship, when we fail to meet our expectations in regard to an exam or to gain a promotion.

At such times, we pass through a period of mourning when we feel a mixture of feelings that we call grief. Following each loss, there is change and in many changes there is gain, but we rarely welcome the change nor see the gain at the time we are grieving.

When we move house, however pleased we are at the thought of the new house, we are sorry to lose the familiar surroundings of our old home. Even after a redundancy, we may find opportunities opening up that actually change our lives for the better. But at the time of the redundancy the future may well have seemed bleak. A child may look forward to a new 'big' school, but still find himself/herself missing nursery school.

Bereavement is a particular loss – one brought about by death. How we as individuals mourn depends on our previous experiences of loss and separation, how we learned to handle our feelings then, and on the support we received. Even the separation and loss felt by infants as they are weaned may have an effect on how they cope with later separations and losses.

Parents – and all adults in charge of children – can make a vital difference to children by the way in which we support them in each time of change or loss.

BEREAVEMENT AND TRADITIONAL PRACTICES

In primitive societies, and even into the twentieth century, there were well-established rituals and rites which supported individuals at times of major life changes. Such rites and rituals had a social expression, but in most communities also were associated with spiritual beliefs.

Social and Religious Practices

In Victorian times, when someone died, the curtains or shutters were drawn in the windows of the house, indicating to passers-by that a death had occurred. Black was worn by women for a year following a close family bereavement, and black armbands were sometimes worn by men. After a death, the body was laid out and friends and neighbours would visit to pay respects and offer condolences. There may have been a vigil with relatives sitting by the body through the night. Children would have been involved in the visiting, and would also be required to wear mourning.

The funeral rites and rituals also followed a prescribed form: the slow procession, the wearing of black or dark colours by all mourners, the service and burial and the refreshments tended to be of similar format for all funerals.

Such rites and rituals made it easier for a grieving person to move through the mourning process. There may have been times specifically set aside for family members to sit silently in grief, accepting the condolences of others; or specific times for family or communal wailing. Then there were often times for the community of family and friends to express their grief together in the traditional funeral and burial ceremonies. Frequently, there were more informal times for the sharing of memories and funeral refreshments. The accepted structures in each community helped those experiencing differing levels of grief to know how to be together, and to support each other.

Children in many cultures have traditionally taken part in both the social and religious practices as a matter of course.

As a consequence of the high mortality rate during childbirth and infancy in Victorian times, children would have been familiar with death in the family as a part of their lives, and they participated fully in all the funeral rites and rituals. They experienced the feelings of grief as normal, and the various rites gave permission and structure to enable grief to be addressed.

Bereavement in the 1990s

In some countries and communities, formalised practices relating to food, drink and clothing still persist. However, our diverse society encompasses a wide range of acceptable values and beliefs. Many of us no longer have the same definite guidelines provided by rituals to support us at times of bereavement. We do not know what form to follow and often have to make difficult decisions at a time when we are grieving. In the struggle to deal with the practicalities, we have less time to acknowledge our own grief or to have others acknowledge it.

More of us today suffer a first personal bereavement in our fifties or sixties when our own parents die. With little experience of loss, we may not expect the feelings of bereavement to be so powerful and confusing. We have lost the understanding of the feelings inherent in normal grief and, rather than allowing ourselves to grieve, we may seek to deny our feelings, using business, alcohol or medication to do so.

In all this, children's needs are often not seen, or are denied. It is assumed that, as one mother said, '. . . *they will soon get over it – children are resilient*,' or, as yet another parent insisted, '. . . *they will not understand . . . we don't want to upset them*.' So children are kept away from the funeral and other ceremonies and sometimes are not even told what has happened.

The Risks of Not Acknowledging Feelings
If we deny our feelings, or those of our children, it is at the risk of having to pay a high price later. Our feelings are a more primitive and basic part of us than our logical thought processes. If we block the expression of our grief, the grief may emerge at a later date as physical symptoms or emotional difficulties. Because of the delay, they may be harder to work through.

The actual expression of grief will differ with each individual. What matters is that the individual should have the opportunity to acknowledge and express it in his/her own way, and not have his/her grief blocked by the demands of others.

NORMAL REACTIONS TO BEREAVEMENT

Adults' Grief – How Long Does the Time of Mourning Last?
Current thinking is that it takes about three years for a 'normally' grieving adult to pass completely through a period of mourning. Although the grief in many people is most intense during the first few months, there are people for whom the second year seems harder than the first. The death of someone close always leaves some residue of sadness, but it need not leave incapacitating feelings that interfere with the ability to engage fully with life once again. This will happen more quickly if mourning is supported rather than blocked.

Grief and Memory

Grief for someone who was close will often be felt again more intensely on anniversaries, holidays and other significant days. This is different from the incapacitating feelings of the initial mourning period – the grief will be re-awakened for a short time. There will also be times when a place, an object, a piece of music or the spoken word will similarly bring memories and briefly re-awaken grief. This is natural and normal for both adults and children who have experienced a loss.

Difficult Bereavements

There are factors that may delay or prolong the grief process. These may be within the personality or upbringing of the mourner who may feel inhibited and unable to express his/her feelings. Other factors are external: if the relationship of the mourner with the person who has died was ambivalent, grief may be prolonged beyond three years; a sudden or traumatic death may similarly lengthen grieving, as may a death before time – that of a child or young person.

Certain intervening factors can delay grieving, for instance, where there are prior emotional factors that demand attention. Thus a pregnant woman or a woman with young children may not be able to grieve until later. Another factor which often leads to an interruption of grieving is the involvement in complex legal or practical matters relating to the bereavement. For some people, this will merely increase the time before the grief work is done. For others, it may result in an inability to grieve, and the individual may become so preoccupied with litigation that they are unable to complete the grieving process.

Children's Grief
In certain respects children's grief is different. Immediately following a significant bereavement, a child may go through a shorter period of mourning than that experienced by adults. However, subsequently, the child may still need to revisit and work through his/her grief at critical stages in his/her physical, emotional and social development.

Maureen, whose mother died when she was five years old, received good family support following the death, and grieved normally at the time.

She became strongly aware of missing her mother again when, as a teenager, she became involved with her first serious boyfriend, and later again when she married. However, Maureen grieved her mother most intensely after the birth of her first baby: she found herself repeatedly waking early, crying, aware of having dreamed. She felt unable to get up, and experienced intense yearning.

Another way in which children differ from adults in their mourning is that they are able to move in and out of grieving regularly throughout the longer process. One moment they may be crying, the next playing happily. Because of this, those adults caring for a bereaved child may think the child is unfeeling, or is at other times 'putting it on'. In actuality, it is just the way that children cope.

Research indicates that experiencing a significant

bereavement before the age of ten can lead to depression in later life, if the grief is not acknowledged, expressed and worked through. It has also been shown that the level of support which a bereaved child receives is the major factor in enabling the child to move normally through the grieving process. Any help that you can provide will make a difference.

Patterns of Reactions to Bereavement
Bereavement encompasses emotional, physical, intellectual, social and spiritual components. It is a deep and complex reaction. Adults and children often feel confused and frightened by the experience. Knowing what is 'normal' can lessen the fear for you and the whole family.

While there is a wide range of normal reactions to a bereavement, every individual, adult or child grieves differently within this spectrum of normality. It is helpful to know what can be 'normal', but equally unhelpful to impose expectations of symptoms and behaviour on our own children. To make a comparison, we know what the symptoms of pregnancy can be, but not all pregnant women experience sickness or cravings for strawberries!

If you are concerned about any reactions your child is showing, check with your GP. There may be reasons for them other than the bereavement. If they are a reaction to the bereavement, the symptoms will pass in time, as the grief is expressed and the child regains a sense of security.

Normal Physical Reactions to a Bereavement
Several of these symptoms may be evident following a bereavement, and it is rare that none of them are. They may not all be present at one time, and each individual will vary both as to duration and intensity with which the reactions are experienced:

- Tearfulness
- Sleep difficulties
- Eating difficulties
- Changes in energy level
- Tensions and pains in different parts of the body
- Increase in intense dreaming
- Regression
- Sensing the presence of the dead person

How a Parent can Help
Accept that what your child is experiencing is genuine. In some ways, it can be as if the body itself feels the grief and needs comforting. Offer solace in the form of additional cuddles, rest, or comforting but healthy food to tempt the appetite. Gently talk about any regression in behaviour (such as thumb-sucking or clinginess) and let the child know that it is fine for now, but that in time he/she will regain confidence; encourage the child to talk of dreams or any sense of the presence of the dead person, and let him/her know that these are normal reactions that will pass.

Normal Intellectual Reactions to a Bereavement
These reactions may be noticed, especially in the school situation, and can interfere with progress:

- Inability to concentrate
- Poor memory
- Lack of interest and motivation
- Repeated need to talk about the dead person
- Questioning all aspects of the death

How a Parent can Help

Give plenty of time to being with and listening to your child. Answer questions as openly as you can. Always notify the school if there is a close bereavement in the family or among friends. Let your child know that you are doing so. Ask the school to let all teachers who are in contact with your child know of the bereavement. Discuss with your child which, if any, of the pupils should be told, and ask the school to go along with the child's wishes. Ask the school to note on all test and exam entries and records that there has been a bereavement. If there are public exams in the offing, consider postponing these. Try to help your child remember his/her homework and the necessary school equipment. You may want to discuss this with the school if he/she continues to forget things. All major decisions about his/her schooling should be deferred if possible.

Normal Emotional Reactions to Bereavement

We are used to the idea that bereavement brings sadness, but we are less aware of the other reactions which bereaved people may experience. This may mean that if a child is not actually spending a lot of time looking sad or crying, the adults caring for the child may not be aware that he/she is, nevertheless, grieving. Also, some of the emotional reactions that the child exhibits may be seen as awkwardness or naughtiness, rather than arising from a genuine need. The most common reactions are feelings of:

- Numbness
- Sadness
- Anger
- Guilt
- Fear
- Isolation/loneliness/feeling 'different' to others
- Helplessness and hopelessness
- Despair

How a Parent can Help
Try to give plenty of time to being with your child. Encourage talk, listen to your child and allow the child his/her feelings, however different to yours. Never dismiss feelings as silly. Share your feelings about the bereavement, possibly explaining why it is good to do so, but also be aware that some of your reactions may not be appropriate for you to share with your child, and that if he/she sees you constantly overwhelmed, he/she may feel extra vulnerable. So, find adult support for yourself. Encourage other family members and adult friends to spend time with the child – there may be things that he/she may want to say but cannot bring himself/herself to say to you. The other family members can reinforce your good work.

Normal Spiritual Reactions to Bereavement
While this is more easily evident in children who have

a religious faith, almost all children faced with a significant bereavement become concerned to explore ideas about an afterlife. Even those children who come from atheist or agnostic homes will have heard religious ideas about God or gods expressed outside the home.

Spiritual reactions may be:

- Feelings of pointlessness – loss of meaning and purpose
- Feelings of emptiness
- Concerns about the nature of existence and an afterlife
- Increase or decrease in commitment to faith

How a Parent can Help
Allow time for the child to talk of these feelings and reactions, and to explore them. Make sure your views are not dogmatic and do not negate his/hers. Develop your own home-based rituals of grieving – fresh flowers by a photograph, a quiet, family, five-minute remembering time every day. Ritual speaks deeply at all transition times, offering security, helping to say goodbye to the old, establishing space to grieve and so encouraging it. Quiet walks in natural settings and an appreciation of beauty soothes the troubled sense of emptiness.

Normal Social Reactions to Bereavement
The inner confusion and intensity a bereaved child experiences tends to be reflected in social interactions. And the fact that he/she is behaving differently may

affect the behaviour of others towards the child. Other children may give up on a child who has become withdrawn or on a child who becomes very quarrelsome. A child who is constantly seeking attention inappropriately may alienate even the best-intentioned teachers. All this compounds the confusion felt by the grieving child. A child who is anxious about leaving a grieving parent alone at home may refuse to go to school and then lose his/her friends at school, and more easily become vulnerable to teasing and isolation. Reactions may include:

- Withdrawal and isolation (whether unconsciously or deliberately)
- Attention seeking
- School refusal

How a Parent can Help
You need to hold the balance between allowing reactions to be expressed in feelings and action, and limiting the negative or detrimental actions. Give your child plenty of attention, and ask others similarly to do so. Be firm about limits to inappropriate attention seeking – distinguish between the feelings and the behaviour – and explain your actions. Seek opportunities for your child to express feelings appropriately. Similarly, allow some time off school, but then insist that the child returns. Let the child know that you have other adult support and that it is not appropriate for him/her to miss school to be at home. Mention any support network that the school can provide. Let your child know which teachers have the

relevant skills, or if there are other agencies that you could contact on his/her behalf for counselling support, or that he/she could contact.

ESPECIALLY DIFFICULT BEREAVEMENTS

Certain sorts of bereavement are by their nature harder for the grieving person to work through than others. This may result in a difficulty in facing the bereavement because, emotionally, it is just too hard to do so. Grief may then be delayed, or it may be that the mourning process is of a longer duration than usual, or it may be that the intensity of the grief itself is felt more deeply.

Hearing Suddenly and Unexpectedly of a Death
For adults, this generally follows a sudden death. This may be the case for children, but there are more cases when news of a death comes to a child unexpectedly. This may be because it was not thought appropriate to warn the child that an illness was likely to be fatal, or the adults have not managed to bring themselves to tell the child, or perhaps they have told the child but the child has not been able to take in the information. (See Chapter Four for Breaking Bad News.)

Deaths in Traumatic Circumstances
These deaths are mostly by accident, for instance, as a result of a major disaster, or by violence. With such deaths, not only the suddenness but the heightened air of dramatic tragedy in the discussions among adults, or possible media attention, can accentuate the emotional

context. The child may be frightened by contact with traumatised adults and, at the same time, less attention may be paid to the child.

In this situation it can be helpful for a child to spend some time with adults whom the child knows well but who are less upset. This will provide some valuable respite from the trauma for the child.

Unmentionable Deaths
Deaths of those in situations which may be unacceptable to a particular family or to society at large may be difficult to grieve. This could occur, for example, where a member of the family dies who has been cut off from the wider family.

Children from divorced or separated families, who may in essence have 'lost' a parent once through divorce, may find difficulty in grieving that dead parent, as they may feel disloyal in confiding in the other partner. The death may also bring up the feelings of loss experienced at the time of the initial separation.

Similar difficulty may occur where there has been a gay relationship, or where the dead person has had AIDS, or where death has been by suicide. In such cases, there may be much kept secret from a child, and the child may sense this yet be unable to ask questions, or to express his/her feelings.

Parents need to balance the benefits of being open with a child against the level of a child's understanding, and the prejudice which the child may encounter if such information inadvertently becomes public. Each situation will be different. It is important, in order to maintain the child's trust, not to be dishonest and to be aware of the likelihood of further information reaching the child from another source. As the child matures parents will want to let him/her know full facts.

Death Before Time
Such deaths can be extremely hard to grieve – they are the deaths of a young person, or someone whom you could rightly expect to live longer. Under this heading could be classed both deaths of children, and also the deaths of parents of children and young people. It is part of our expectation that our parents will live long enough to bring us to adulthood, and we do not expect children to die.

It is hard for a child to accept the death of another child, and very frightening. The nature of the illness or the accident should be carefully explained many times, to put into perspective the child's fears that he/she may also die soon.

Death Following a Long and Stressful Illness
Where an adult has been involved, over a period of time, with a terminally ill person, though the death has been expected and some preliminary grieving done, he/she may be emotionally and physically exhausted by the time the actual death occurs.

For a child who has been part of a household in which a very sick person has been nursed, or where there have been long-term demands of hospital visits, the situation is also hard. Such a child will have been living with the stresses of the adults for that time, and without the quantity and quality of attention that would be usual. In a sense, the child may have been deprived of a considerable chunk of carefree childhood, and there may be a whole raft of feelings of grief because of this, as well as those belonging to the actual bereavement.

In such a case, the child is going to need and benefit from as much adult (preferably parental) attention as possible, and probably the listening ear of a non-involved adult. The child will need emotional rest, permission and encouragement to play and to be a child, and to be allowed to express any resentment for the time and attention he/she has lost. This may not just be resentment towards the parent who has been unable to give him/her this attention, but it can also be towards the dead person.

How a Parent can Help in all Difficult Bereavements
Because the process of grieving may be harder in these cases, it is important that you observe carefully whether and how the child is grieving and, if in doubt, call for professional help. The child may need help that you, because of your own grief, are unable to give, and there is a wide range of help available in many communities. (See Chapter Eight and Appendices.)

Importance of the Nature of the Relationship

It is important to recognise that, just as the nature of each relationship between individuals is different, so grieving will differ according to the formal relationship between the child and the deceased person. The death of a pet, for instance, may be felt very strongly by a child, although some adults may find this hard to understand.

Death of a Parent
In many cases, the death of a parent will have the most consequences. Not only will the mourning be more intense, but the developmental consequences of not having a parent as a model, or as practical and emotional support through your childhood and young adolescence, poses particular difficulties. There will also be fear that the surviving parent may die as well.

How a Parent Can Help
The grieving child will need increased support from the remaining parent, yet often the surviving parent, who is himself/herself grieving, also becomes emotionally lost to the child. It may also be that a child feels that he/she has to become the carer of the surviving parent or siblings – let him/her know that is not so. Close friends and family are particularly important as compensatory support for a child whose parent dies. An emphasis needs to be put on the fact that there are many caring adults within the community, adults are the carers, not children.

Death of a Sibling
This can be complicated by a child's naturally complex feelings towards siblings. Along with companionship, there is often rivalry – so there may be loneliness and relief and guilt as part of the grief. There may also be feelings that he/she as the surviving child has to be everything for the parents, or has to live for both

himself/herself and the dead sibling. And there is likely to be fear: if it can happen to him/her, it can happen to me.

How a Parent can Help
Let your child be himself/herself; stress differences between him/her and the dead child, being sure you speak of positives of each. It is easy to over-idealise a child that has died. Also, be sure to reiterate that, whatever happened, it was not the surviving child's fault. Even where it is an accident that involves the surviving child, emphasise that the adults concerned carry the responsibility. At the same time, try to avoid being too over-protective, it is not fair on the surviving child if you allow your fears to get in the way of his/her natural development.

Death of a Grandparent
Here the situation depends enormously on what the relationship means to the child.

Charlie (aged seven), whose parents were very busy with work and younger children, had a grandfather who, since Charlie was quite young, had taken him fishing most weekends. When his grandfather died, Charlie missed him deeply and blamed himself for the death. Charlie actually said that he felt his grandfather had given up because Charlie had begun going out with him less often and seeing more of his own friends.

Fiona (aged nine) said, 'I didn't really know my gran well, but my dad said that she was very wise and that I would be able to go and stay with her for holidays when I was older. I really wanted to know her.'

It is not always the case that the most apparently loving and close relationship is the hardest to grieve. In fact, it is often the 'harder' relationships, the ones in which there is more ambivalence, that may be more difficult.

Sophie (aged six) found it very hard to grieve for her very critical grandmother. A year after the death, Sophie would wake crying from nightmares in which her grandmother appeared, shouting that Sophie must not eat with her mouth open.

How Parents can Help

Whatever your parent or in-law meant to you, remember that your child has had a different relationship with him/her. Show that you value the differences between your relationships. While you may not particularly have liked your father-in-law, your child may have loved him deeply (or the other way round). If you can approach this as one of the strengths and wonders of family life, it will help the child to express what he/she needs to.

Death of a Friend

When a friend dies a child may grieve more deeply than a parent can easily understand. Children can become very attached to their friends in an emotional and practical way, especially while at school. During the business of a school day, this can be a strong bond that helps a child to cope in a large group.

A parent, seeing how upset a child becomes when a

friend dies, may feel bewildered, that the child is 'putting it on', or even a little jealous. This may be heightened if the grieving child spends a lot of time with the dead child's family.

Shirley (aged sixteen) found it very hard to get over her friend Linda's sudden death from asthma. 'I need to be with her mum, just now. My mum isn't feeling anything. She doesn't know how Linda helped me. She stood by me when I was bullied at primary school.'

How a Parent can Help
Your child may need extra help and support of the kind his/her former friend provided. So listen carefully to him/her, let him/her grieve. He/she may sense any jealousy you feel towards the friend's parents – acknowledge this and let him/her know that you also appreciate the generosity he/she is showing.

Death of a Pet
The sense of emotional support, companionship and affection given to a child by a pet means that the loss can be sadly felt.

How a Parent can Help
Acknowledge the death as important to the child, and allow him/her to grieve even if you do not feel sad. We as adults can help a child by really honouring the need for a respectful ending and burial, with the child having as much choice as possible over the arrangements. Some local authorities do now provide special areas where pets can be buried.

STAGES OF GRIEVING

While every child will exhibit different symptoms at different times during the process of bereavement, there is a recognisable sequence of reactions that many pass through. In some ways, this is more like a route of grief along which the individual travels, but he/she may need to go back and revisit points on the route several times.

Stages of Grieving

On hearing of a bereavement:
- Shock, panic
- Numbness
- Disbelief

Expression of very mixed feelings including:
- Denial and searching activity
- Anger
- Fear
- Guilt
- Despair

Coping behaviour, but without real interest:
- Taking part in previous activities
- Initiating some new activities

Reinvestment:
- Looking forward again
- Involvement in life with zest and energy

How a Parent can Help

Although there is this common sequence of movement through the mourning process, your support is crucial in helping your child move through his/her grief. It is not so much helping him/her to move faster than he/she naturally can, but rather, helping by allowing him/her to be where he/she is with the grief and keeping the grieving track well oiled and free of obstacles.

Because you know what is normal, you can let him/her know that it is valuable to express what he/she needs to express, but in a way that is safe to do so.

You can build into his/her life additional opportunities for the grieving to manifest itself, and accept when he/she needs to 'play'.

You can listen to him/her with acceptance, even though your feelings may be different to his/hers. Enlist other adults to listen and, if he/she is a teenager, friends of his/her own age also.

Chapter Two
CHILDREN'S THINKING ABOUT BEREAVEMENT AND LOSS

Each child is an individual who will move through different stages of development at his/her own pace. But a child will also be affected by what happens in his/her life. While there have been a number of studies suggesting how children will respond to a bereavement at any stage of development and maturity, there is only a general agreement between these studies as to whether a particular mode of thinking belongs to a particular age or stage of a child's development or to the preceding or following stage. Consequently, while we can suggest reactions your child is likely to show at a particular age, they may, in fact, differ for any number of reasons.

It is also worth bearing in mind that, where studies have been based on interviews with children who have been bereaved as opposed to non-bereaved children, the results may differ considerably. The effects of a bereavement may cause a child to regress to a younger level of thinking, just as a child will regress behaviourally to thumb-sucking or bed-wetting. However, knowing something about how normal thinking about death and bereavement develops may give some indication as to when a child has completed grieving as far as can be expected for his/her age.

Conversely, it will indicate when a child is stuck at a younger level of thinking than one might expect. If you are concerned that this might be so, do seek professional help from a bereavement counsellor. (See Chapter Eight and Appendix A.)

BEREAVEMENT ISSUES AND A CHILD'S THINKING

Life experience frames our understanding and reactions to all losses. The infant's sense of being an individual as separate from his/her mother, the understanding that people temporarily out of sight still continue to exist, the capacity to think in concepts and plan for a future are learned as a child matures.

Bereavement, being a permanent loss, raises particular issues for the child to think about. The loss may cause particular difficulties, according to the development of the child's thought processes. Whether the loss is permanent, the meaning of death, distinctions between body and soul, and who, if anyone, carries responsibility for death will all be particular issues at different stages.

Along with these questions go issues more related to practicalities, and the child's knowledge of the world and relationships. Who will care for whom? Where will the money come from?

The child's emotional response will interact with his/her intellectual response. If a child thinks that he/she did something bad and that this caused his/her sibling's death (however unrealistic this is), he/she will feel guilty.

EARLY CHILDHOOD:
4 – 7 YEARS OLD

An infant's thoughts will gradually organise themselves through the stage of recognising that certain objects, animals and people have names and have some measure of constancy that can be recognised. He/she will also learn that there is security and safety in the presence and reliability of his/her caretakers, and that he/she, the infant, can control parts of the environment himself/herself, and those around him/her. But there is no objective understanding of why this is so – just that it is so.

At four years old, a child's thought processes are still egocentric. He/she will have difficulty in perceiving situations through another's viewpoint, and essentially will see the world as centred on himself/herself and his/her needs. The child has an immature sense of logic in a way that has been called 'magical' because of the intuitive quality of some of the cause and effect connections that he/she makes, often ascribing to inanimate objects a variety of thoughts, feelings and deliberate actions. He/she will have difficulty in conceiving of the absolute ending of a human or animal life. A child's real understanding is still based on what is concrete and actual to his/her senses. He/she will only have a limited sense of time in terms of duration. For instance, he/she may know the days of the week but is unlikely to be able to think far ahead.

THINKING ABOUT DEATH IN EARLY CHILDHOOD: 4 – 7 YEARS OLD

The following reactions may be seen:

Illogical Self-blame
He/she may illogically take on responsibility when things go wrong in the family and others are upset. When there is a bereavement, he/she may link this to his/her own sense of 'badness', or even to a time when he/she felt 'bad' in relation to the person who has died.

William (aged five), whose teenage sister had died in a road accident, needed to keep repeating that she was a bad girl running in front of the bus, and reassuring himself that he had looked both ways. He needed to know that he wasn't bad. Understanding adults were able to reassure him that he was not responsible for his sister and that her death was not his fault.

Selina (aged eight) had been alone in the house with her father when he had a fatal heart attack. She was very concerned with what she could have done to upset him. He had been displeased with her school report the previous week, and she had answered back rudely when he had criticised her. She 'magically' thought that her rudeness might have been the cause of his death. While the adults in Selina's life did what they could to reassure her, and explained about heart attacks, she was left with vestiges of self-blame even as an adult.

Denial/Wishful Thinking

Magical thought will also show itself in the denial following a death, where the magic lies in believing that what is wished might come true.

Alice (aged seven) invented a fantasy that her mother had not really died but that she had gone to live somewhere else because she was not happy with the family, and that she and Alice would meet years later. All this, in spite of the fact that Alice had been taken to see her dead mother, a mother who had known she was dying and had written a goodbye letter for Alice to keep.

Death Seen as Temporary.
Afterlife Seen in Concrete Terms

Some children at this stage of development may still see death as temporary, thinking 'heaven' is another place from which the dead person will return. The child may have a lot of assumptions, for instance, that the dead person will continue to grow.

'What will Sheila think of me being in her bedroom now?' asked Philip (aged seven). And later, 'Will I have to move out when she comes back?'

Interest in Concrete Meaning of Death

There may be considerable interest in dead bodies, for instance, of dead pets or small wild creatures or insects. Animals may be buried and then uncovered by the child so that he/she can check on what is happening. What does being dead really mean?

Simon (aged seven) showed his concern as to what happened after death in his pictures of his father. He drew him 'dirty' because of the earth that Simon knew had been piled on top of the coffin.

Personification of Death, Sometimes in Frightening Form.
Fears of Death Happening in Sleep

Because of their tendency to personify, children at this age may also imagine death as a person who will come and get them. They may be frightened at night, and become afraid of going to sleep, especially if an adult has compared death and sleep. Or they may be frightened of a surviving parent being taken away by death.

Their thinking may also occasionally be further complicated if there is a spiritual framework within the family. If a child does not understand phrases such as 'Going to heaven' or 'The angels coming to take you', he/she will create his/her own images, which may be worrying to him/her.

Vicky (aged six) was concerned about how the angels would be able to get the body of her mother out of the coffin if it had been nailed down.

It can also be hard for children to come to terms with what has been explained to them in the past as a caring deity who then takes a loved one away. Again, a child may think God is angry with them for something that they have done wrong.

THE MIDDLE YEARS: 8 – 12 YEARS OLD

During this stage, children start to move slowly towards understanding ideas that depend less on concrete physical examples and are more abstract ways of thinking. They begin to understand longer and wider perspectives on life, having a greater understanding of future and of past time, and a sense of permanent separations and endings. But, for much of this stage, they may be more interested in collecting facts than in thinking abstractly. They have a rather black-and-white mentality: judgements tend to be made on the basis of fairness according to set rules that they have heard and accepted or formulated for themselves. At this stage, it is natural for children to be concerned with activities and competencies.

Need for Factual Information

Children in the middle years will have many factual questions to ask about loss, if they are given the opportunity to do so. They are likely to want to know what caused a death. They actually want to go into the concrete details. And they will, if given the chance, check several times to make sure they really do understand what is meant.

Delroy (aged twelve), whose father died of lung cancer, went over and over with many adults the details of how cancer develops and what happens when someone has cancer. He wanted to know why one smoker gets cancer while another does not, whether it is painful, and what radiotherapy and chemotherapy are. Not all of these questions could be answered with certainty.

Children may also want to know the details of what happens at a funeral or cremation. Particularly in regard to cremation, if a child is not given the chance to ask questions, or is not given answers, he/she is likely to construct his/her own fantasy around the situation. This may be not only be inaccurate, but more difficult to accept than the truth.

At this age, there is also a greater tendency for psychosomatic symptoms to develop following death. It may be because the child cannot fully understand why it is that a particular illness has developed in the person who has died; or it may be a form of over-identification with the dead person.

Susan (aged twelve), who had never fainted before, began fainting regularly after her father died from a heart attack.

Rachel (aged ten) started taking time away from school with very real-feeling stomach aches after her father died of stomach cancer.

Need for Fairness.
Rigid Rules such as 'Only Old People Die'
The unfairness of death is felt very strongly at this stage: why should it happen to them, to me? It should just be old people.

'She didn't look ill – she came to tea the day before she died – she didn't have a chance,' was a comment that Trish (aged nine) still made months after the death of her aunt.

'How come she got leukemia? She wasn't very old,' said Angela (aged ten).

Concerns about Practicalities
Issues around finance and practical support arise at this stage, insecurity is expressed most strongly in regard to money and food.

'My brother hasn't got a lot of money – he can't pay for me.' Francis (aged eleven).

TEENAGERS: 12 – 18 YEARS OLD

By the age of eleven, many young people can think in the abstract, and enjoy doing so. They have a more sophisticated sense of future, and think in an increasingly reasoned, systematic and sustained manner.

Concurrently, teenagers may increasingly be more independent of parents in an everyday sense, and relate more easily and regularly to their peers. They often behave as if they feel capable and powerful, yet underneath this may be an underlying feeling of lack of knowledge and experience.

Teenagers often concern themselves with matters of identity, and seek for ideals to relate to. It is a time for exploring new areas of life and thought, often questioning the values espoused by their parents.

Because it is so much a time for the new, it poses particular difficulties for a teenager who is bereaved. The teenager is pulled between the grief for the person who has died and is truly in the past, and the natural developmental tasks of exploring new territory.

Using Peer Group Support

This can work very well, so long as there are sufficient friends to draw upon. If a bereaved teenager depends too much upon one other teenager, it can ultimately become too much of a burden and destroy the friendship. Parents may feel cut off if a teenager chooses to share his/her grief mainly with friends. It may help to recognise that this peer support can be healthy in the long term, and in a sense it is a way of keeping the teenager's forward movement in life, rather than regressing to earlier dependency on the family.

Questioning Meaning and Values

Death can mean a complete turn-about in a teenager's attitude and behaviour. It can either cause a light-hearted teenager to adopt a deeper attitude to life, or conversely lead an earnest, studious teenager to give up his/her academic aspirations.

Following the death of his father from a heart attack in his early forties, James (aged fifteen) became very introspective, questioning the point of all the effort he had been putting into his schoolwork – if this is all life is and you can die any time, why bother?

Understanding of Long-Term Practical Implications

It should be remembered that, along with a fast maturing sense of values, teenagers are at a stage where they can consider the long-term implications of decisions that they may be called upon to make. For instance, a bereavement at a time when there are major exams calls for a decision that can only be made by the teenager – whether, because of his/her current feelings of grief, to postpone the exams, or whether he/she does not feel too overwhelmed and can still manage to prepare adequately for them (in which case, ask the school to let the examination boards know of the bereavement). Each individual's situation and decision would be different, and if they do decide to focus on exams, it is important that they allot a future time for grieving. You should also let the teenager know that if at any time they feel they cannot cope, this is fine – they have the options. Not every teenager, nor every adult, would want to make or be able to follow through on a decision, as in the following example:

Rachel, who was seventeen when her parents both died, made a conscious decision to immerse herself in her work, but promised herself she would do her grieving when she had finished her exams – and was able to do so. She said years later that she knew that if she had let herself grieve at the time of her parents' death, she would never have been able to complete her studies. She had a grasp of the long-term implications of the bereavement, and the capacity to manage her feelings until she had got the time and energy to grieve.

Over-responsible Behaviour
Because teenagers can seem so mature and able to cope, they are at times given too many heavy responsibilities by the family after a close death. This

can mean that they are not able to pass through their natural developments, nor through the natural grieving process. For instance, a teenager who is asked to fill the parental role of a parent who has died may years later find himself/herself living a delayed teenage rebellious stage.

James (aged eighteen) was a source of strength for over a year to the family of his best friend who was killed in a road accident. James did everything for this family: went shopping for the mother, helped the younger children with homework, serviced the car with the father. Finally, it was too much. With no warning, he walked out on his home and college course.

Interest in the Spiritual/Supernatural
As part of the natural questioning of what death and life mean, teenagers often become particularly interested in religion or in the supernatural. This can lead to fervent espousal of a particular religious group, or even to an interest in less traditionally acceptable areas.

Catlin (aged seventeen) became fascinated by the supernatural when her mother died. She read widely around the subject and then began experimenting with the ouija board. With support and understanding from her school, she eventually found the spiritual help she needed through a church.

How a Parent can Help at all Stages
- Continue to be there. Your presence will be supportive, even if a teenager appears not to

need you to express his/her grief.

- Speak of the dead person, thus specifically allowing the death to be discussed, and lessening the tendency for denial.
- Listen to facts and views, and especially to feelings, taking them seriously, even if they seem irrational or are different to yours.
- Offer factual information, to help the teenager dispell illogical guilt, wistful thinking and irrational fears.
- Discuss your views of death and allow for discussion of other views.
- Accept the support of others.

Chapter Three
PREPARING A CHILD FOR LOSSES AND CHANGES

To prepare your child for the changes, losses and bereavements which he/she will inevitably experience, you need to consider how a child learns, and how you can help in this process.

FEELINGS AND LEARNING

Children learn best when their need to do so is aroused by curiosity, or if their feelings or interest are triggered. (Although, if feelings are too strongly triggered so that a child is overexcited or frightened, he/she may be unable to learn.)

The feelings themselves are innate in all of us. The only thing children have to learn is how to use these feelings. Children need to learn:

- To talk about and express their feelings
- When to express feelings appropriately
- The inner tools of how to handle feelings so that they neither overwhelm us (as in a two-year-old's tantrums) nor get suppressed, resurfacing later as antisocial behaviour or depression

Importance of How You Communicate

Listening to Your Child

Listening is a skill that is of help in all relationships. Learning to listen both to the facts and also to feelings is of utmost importance. In the traumatic instance of the loss of a pet, the facts may be simple. The cat has disappeared. But to the cat's owner, whether adult or child, the feelings are intense. Adults learn to manage these feelings and emotions so as to be able to get on with what needs doing. But we may forget to listen to and validate a child's feelings. A child may then feel unheard, and confused that the feelings that may be so strong to him/her are apparently not important to the adult. The child then may feel somehow 'wrong'. Simply listening and acknowledging the child's feelings is a crucial skill for a parent to acquire.

Communicating Your Feelings

From his/her birth onwards, you have been teaching your child to communicate. But some parents find it hard to specifically encourage the communication of feelings. The way most parents do this is by being a role-model for their child, showing him/her that it is all right to feel happy and sad, pleased and angry, bored and . . . whatever. As you do this and speak of how you feel, you help the child to develop a wide vocabulary through which to express his/her own feelings. More than this, by allowing your child to see that feelings are acceptable, and showing him/her how to express them appropriately, you will be affirming his/her self-esteem.

At a time of loss, when the ability to express feelings is so important, the fact that you have prepared your child in this way will be invaluable.

Answering Your Child's Questions

In situations of change and loss, encouraging and answering your child's questions in a way that he/she can understand is vital. You need to be prepared to repeat, going over the same ground many times in different ways, as the child tries to take in the information.

One way you can help a child to understand is to give examples of what others sometimes need to ask, or of what others may find difficult.

James (aged five) was very subdued at the first meeting with a counsellor three months after his father's death in an accident. James had begun to refuse to go to school. When he was told by the counsellor that sometimes children wanted to ask questions about what actually happened, or where the dead person is, James became more alert and asked why his dad had died in the accident. He was shown in a concrete way, using flowers on a plant, that there could be slight damage, or complete crushing of the flower from which it could not recover.

James appeared greatly relieved and the counsellor could then explore with him the different ways we use the word 'accident', and how it meant quite a different range of incidents.

It seemed that previously, he had not fully understood the word and had built up fears of accidents at school, but he could not bring himself to ask about them without specific permission to do so. School attendance ceased to be a problem.

Difficulties with Vocabulary and Colloquialisms

Many words or phrases may affect a child in ways we do not anticipate, as in the example above. Parents who describe death as 'going to sleep' may find a child becomes afraid of sleeping. Children may become anxious about dead people being 'taken' to heaven, and become fearful of all sickness in the family. Terms such as 'a heart attack' need to be explained – children have been known to interpret this as someone being stabbed in the heart.

To be more aware of possible misunderstanding, listen for a sequence of questions, or for sudden silences that show a child is trying to grasp something difficult. Asking them to tell you the details of what they think has happened may help you to perceive how much they understand, just as encouraging them to ask questions can also help.

PROVIDING A RICH BREADTH OF EXPERIENCE

As your child develops you need to offer him/her experiences that will interest him/her and that relate to change and loss. This will encourage him/her to ask questions and learn from the experiences. You may be the leader in terms of providing the situation, and the follower in responding to the child's interest. If a neighbour moves, you could focus on the possible changes, for your family and for the neighbours.

Discuss the news with your child, especially in relation to the death of someone famous. British children will be familiar with the Princess of Wales's death. This might be the starting point for a conversation about death. Introduce such subjects, and then let the child's own interest determine the development of the conversation.

THE FOUNDATIONS OF PREPARING A CHILD FOR CHANGE AND LOSS

The preparation you do in the early months of your child's life provides the foundations for all relationship issues. You establish the bond between yourself and your infant wherein the infant feels safe, and then gradually you help him/her to know that even when you do leave him/her you will return. The development of feelings that include a tolerated separation as a natural process are important.

Further preparation for loss and change, through simple ways, will continue to be of value. As your child develops from infant to toddler, so you can continue to prepare for losses and changes in life, both by games you play and through everyday experiences.

Games
Games of hiding and finding all help the child gain experiences of temporary separation, and begin to extend the idea that he/she may not always be in control of when the separation will end. He/she will increasingly learn to tolerate the feelings of loss within a context of overall safety and security in his/her life.

As we play games of hide and seek, we can verbalise the questions for the child: 'Where is Daddy? He is gone, he is hiding.' Then, 'There he is, Daddy is here now.'

Increased Periods of Separation from Mother/Father

You can gradually and in a systematic way increase the length of time your child gets used to being without you. During early childhood you can help ease the feelings of loss a child experiences by leaving him/her in familiar surroundings, with other familiar people, and with a favourite toy or blanket which provides a link with you.

Developing Patterns of Parting and Meeting

As a part of this, you will again almost naturally establish patterns or rituals of parting. Through these, there is a gradually built-up feeling of safety about parting, as the child knows how it will happen.

The goodnight kiss and the action of tucking the child safely into bed, accompanied by familiar, repeated phrases, gives the child a regular and reliable experience of the feelings at the moment of parting. The doorstep goodbyes to family and friends, also with kisses, hugs and waves, acknowledges the pleasure of having spent time together, and the sadness at parting.

It is important with the regular partings that there is also a reassurance as to your return. A child at this stage will probably not be able to tell the time, but it will be helpful for you to say that you will be back for tea, or bath-time, to give the child something to hang on to. Then it will be important for you to do all you can to keep to that commitment.

On your return, the greetings will also become part of a pattern that you establish. As before, the pleasure in being together again can be acknowledged and shared. This regular way of separating and returning will help your child realise that feelings of sadness and sometimes anger at parting, and of pleasure and relief at meeting again, are all safe ones to have.

'You haven't said, "Goodnight, sleep tight",' said Neil (aged three). 'I can't go to sleep yet.'

STARTING PLAYGROUP OR SCHOOL

In the earliest years, experiences of parting generally involve the child still being left in familiar situations with familiar people in family-sized groups. Beginning playgroup or school will invariably be significantly different. It will be a larger environment, where there are likely to be more children and less opportunity for a close relationship with, or close attention from, the adult in charge. Again, you can prepare your child in many ways:

• Several visits before beginning school can be helpful, so that the way there, the school building, the sight of mothers and children going in, become familiar. Most nurseries and schools invite parents and new children to a preliminary visit in the building to see where everything is and ask questions.

You can prepare children further at home by:

- Talking in more detail about what it will be like – reminding him/her of where the lavatories are, and the coat pegs, and what the lunch arrangements are.
- Playing make-believe playgroup with the child and with his/her toys.
- Providing your child with familiar 'linking objects' – a schoolbag perhaps, or a tiny teddy bear for his/her pocket. Just knowing he/she has it there will help him/her to feel safe.
- Especially important will be to talk through what it will be like when you actually leave him/her, and about the feelings you will both have; also talk about what you will do when he/she is not at home, and where you will collect him/her and what you will do then.

Nature and Changes

The natural cycle, too, will help a child experience change as normal and healthy. Plants and flowers within your home, in the garden or parks can show a child not just natural growth and change but give early notions of death. Seasonal changes from bud break to leaf fall, and planting seeds and bulbs can all be used.

The vital ingredient is that the child is offered the experience and that you should talk about it together – that ideas and feelings are expressed and questions answered honestly.

Experiences at Second-hand – Books and Videos

There are many excellent picture books, poems and

even videos that deal with loss and change, and which provide an excellent means of preparing a child.

It is not just the experience of having the book read to him/her that is important, but the talk as you do so, encouraging the child to make personal links between his/her experience and the story. While reading John Burningham's *Grandad* to a child, comparisons can be made to old people whom the child knows. While reading the poem *Alexander Beetle* by A. A. Milne the child can be asked to talk of how he/she feels when he/she loses something. (See Appendix B for other books.)

PREPARING A CHILD OF 5 – 7 YEARS OLD TO DEAL WITH SITUATIONS OF CHANGE AND LOSS

At this stage, a child will be constantly extending experiences of change and loss. How you prepare and support your child as he/she experiences all changes will make a difference. You can continually affirm changes as natural, and the cause of many mixed feelings.

There will not only be more changes and losses, but the child will be dealing with them in increasingly less personal, more formal situations. Yet the changes he/she will be experiencing may be strong ones, so your support as a parent is important.

Time as a Factor in Preparation for Change
You can use the calendar to gradually prepare for parting dates. A child can begin to pace and prepare

himself/herself, acknowledging the last days as well as the last times. For instance, the last time the au pair will spend Christmas with the family, or the last time he/she will take a child swimming, so that a sense of counting down to a final day is experienced.

Involving your Child in Preparing for Change

The more your child is involved in choices and preparations for changes, the easier the change will be. Rather than experiencing helplessness at an inevitable and imposed change, the child will feel some capacity to co-operate with and influence the change.

For a school-aged child there may be changes of teacher, friends or after-school child-minder, au pair or nanny. Give time to talk through what it will be like after the change. If there is to be a present, let your child give his/her own, making or choosing it. Let him/her help to plan a goodbye event, involving all sorts of memories which you can either discuss or make a photo album or scrap book about.

Preparation for Life After the Change or Loss

It can be especially useful to look forward to life after the change in terms of what has been learned before the change that will help in the new.

'I'll always remember Sarah – she helped me to swim. Now I can go to the club each week without her.'

Preparation for Permanent Losses

You can explicitly familiarise your child with the feelings of permanent losses by using everyday opportunities when household objects or clothes need to be discarded. For instance, talk of your mixed feelings as you throw out an old, chipped mug that a schoolfriend gave you when you were a child but that now just clutters the shelf. This will encourage the child also to discard items that he/she no longer uses and to allow himself/herself the mixed feelings that go with this change.

Changes of Friends
Changes in friendships can be hard for a child to deal with – we are not always aware of the depth of attachment and interdependence between childhood friends at school.

Even harder for a child, but often something which is hard to prepare for, are those friendship changes which leave your child feeling rejected. There may be nothing he/she can do to re-awaken the friendship. The only real preparation for this sort of loss is to encourage your child to develop a range of friends, and to participate in a range of activities.

Overnight Separation for Parents
It is during this stage in their development that children will benefit from experiencing overnight and increasingly longer separation from their parents. This may be with another family, or on a club or school trip. Here again, talking it through in advance is invaluable: what happens in Granny's house if I wake up early?

Children often need to know about differences in night-time and household routines – will a light be left on? Can they take a favourite cuddly toy to camp?

Before your child spends time away, check out what will be expected, so that you can be sure to prepare him/her. It can be reassuring for your child to take a special something with him/her – if not a large toy, something little that others may not even know is there.

This preparation is well worth while. If things go wrong during an early overnight separation, subsequent longer separations may be harder.

PREPARING 8 – 12 YEAR OLDS

At this age, children's understanding of the finality of death itself is beginning to develop. Experiences of the natural world will have helped with this. They will already have had some experience through school of natural change and transformations, such as how frogs and butterflies develop. These experiences can be used to provide a real link for them at a stage when their own bodies will also be starting to develop.

The development of butterflies in particular provides a useful analogy for helping the child to understand ideas about the existence of a soul or spirit as distinct from the physical body. The butterfly leaves the cocoon (the body) and lives on in another form (the spirit).

Other opportunities to explore the nature of death are likely to present themselves through dead insects and small wild animals and birds. Your child, in examining the differences between a dead and live creature, can ask questions and talk about what it is to be dead.

Their curiosity about a wider range of facts, their

greater sense of time, and their own skills in accessing information, whether through reading matter or other media, mean that children of this age group have the ability to explore their interests increasingly independently as well as with you.

Death of Pets

The death of a pet, whether at home or school, is very sad for children. It can be mourned in its own right, but such deaths can also be preparation for the death of people. Where a pet is ill, your child should be allowed to participate in its care, if possible. This will help him/her feel that he/she has done something to help, and will alleviate feelings of helplessness. The awareness of good veterinary care also builds another strand of understanding. Treating the body of a dead pet with respect will also be significant. Some local authorities have areas set aside for pets' burials.

Gruesome, Frightening Images

Children may ask many questions about death and dead bodies when they are at this stage. They often focus on seemingly gruesome details. It is a need to know in detail that leads them to prod, poke and dissect dead creatures. It is this concrete interest, allied to a tendency to personalise abstract fears, that can lead to terrifying images of ghosts and monsters.

Where fears do develop, it will help a child to have his/her fears acknowledged, and to let the child know that, while for him/her the images are real and frightening, you do not see them. You need to emphasise that you want to help him/her feel safer.

Leave the light on and the door open for him/her. Help him/her to devise ways of helping himself/herself, for instance, if he/she gets up and has a drink, straightens out his/her sheets and then reads a book, the fears may disappear. Whatever the fears, it is not helpful to encourage the habit of the child sleeping with you.

Maggie (aged eight) was greatly helped to conquer her night-time monsters when her mother encouraged her to make some make-believe dragons to keep the monsters at bay. Maggie drew two large dragons, coloured them brightly and kept the drawings under her bed. She was then able to sleep soundly.

Wider Influences and Differing Spiritual Beliefs
It is bewildering for children today that there is no generally accepted view of death or an afterlife. They hear many conflicting ideas. Issues that may be particularly difficult for parents to deal with and for a child to comprehend are those about the difference between the soul and the body; where the soul goes after death; how it gets out of the coffin or whether, for instance, the soul of a sibling will continue to grow old in the afterlife.

As parents, a useful approach is to be honest and open about your views, which includes letting your child know when you do not know about something. Also, acknowledge that there are people who hold views that are different to your own and that he/she will be able to decide on his/her own views as he/she grows up.

If you are open and honest with your children, they will continue to trust you, ask you questions, share their views and explore issues with you. If a child finds you have been dishonest, it may be hard for him/her to continue to be open with you.

One way of explaining difference is by analogy: you like apples – I prefer oranges. No amount of argument makes us better than each other or persuades us to change what we like.

PREPARING A YOUNG PERSON OF 12 YEARS AND UPWARDS TO COPE WITH CHANGE AND LOSS

Adolescence is a time of many changes – changes within the adolescent and how he/she relates to others. It is also a time which is charged with emotion, when the adolescent needs to explore his/her own identity and values. And it is a time when, in exploring choices of the infinite possibilities that exist in the world, the adolescent experiences a variety of losses. Your adolescent will be capable of thinking and talking about how he/she has coped with past change, so that he/she knows what to expect of himself/herself, but the feelings may still be intense. Particular changes relating to adolescence will be:

Physical Changes
Preparing a pubescent child for physical changes is often a matter of information and reassurance. Be prepared to broach this area frequently – your child may want to talk, but feel reluctant to begin.

Relationship Changes
This is a time when peer group relationships become more important than those within the family. It is also a time when friendships may become more intimate and sexual. Feelings of jealousy and exclusion from others within a group, or arising from changes in relationships, are common.

Changes in Expectations
Young people often face major disappointments in expectations, usually because of examination results. So much emphasis is placed on success that failure can seem almost unbearable and humiliating. In planning for the future, it can help if parents continually encourage an adolescent to think of a range of possible alternative ways forward, so that one way does not become the only way, and failure thus becomes less catastrophic.

Changes in Responsibilities
An adolescent needs to be increasingly independent in all areas of life: not only academic work, but budgeting, self-care and chores, and having to spend some lengthy periods of time away from home with youth groups, foreign exchange visits, or camps. Lack of experience of practical independence can prove a major hazard that interferes with the teenager's ability to settle into higher education or a job, if he/she has not been encouraged to learn the necessary competencies earlier. It is natural that teenagers should resist being asked to take on additional chores when at home. As a parent, tough love means seeing this as

necessary preparation for future change.

How a Parent can Help

• Listen without judging or saying that you warned him/her. If and when he/she finds change difficult, he/she will know that he/she can rely on you in this way.

• Continue to be there. Your adolescent may react against your imposing limits but be glad you have provided them. He/she may not apparently want the benefit of your experience today, and yet be grateful for it next week. When so much else is likely to be changing, your constancy will be supportive.

If the world he/she is exploring and measuring himself/herself against lets him/her down – and this may be in terms of a relationship, or of academic success, or of social success – he/she will need to reassure himself/herself of the security of his/her relationship with you.

Your experience of the range of options available is far wider than that of an adolescent. Encourage him/her not to make decisions and commitments too early, but to be aware that many options are often available.

• Learn when to stand aside. During this stage, an adolescent is often more likely to want to depend on and rely on his/her peer group in day-to-day matters, and even in crisis. It is healthy that he/she should do so – it shows he/she is moving towards becoming an independent adult. Stand back, but be there ready to support if asked. And let him/her know that this is what you are doing.

• Help to build a sense of perspective. When a change is likely to be particularly difficult to handle, remind the adolescent of how other changes have been hard, and how what seemed very important at the time is now no longer so. Adolescents are able to think more clearly and abstractly both about the past and about the future, and this can be of great help.

• You can also use many second-hand experiences, from books or the media, to help him/her to learn in advance about the range of reactions that are part of the normal processes of change and loss.

Chapter Four
BREAKING THE NEWS OF AN ANTICIPATED BEREAVEMENT TO A CHILD OR YOUNG PERSON

The more understanding and well-worked-through the experiences of lesser losses a child or young person has had, the better he/she will be able to cope with a bereavement. However, the anticipated bereavement of a loved one will still be very hard.

There are specific ways that can make an anticipated bereavement easier for the whole family to work through.

When you first hear that a bereavement is likely to occur, you are going to have to make a decision as to when to tell the child, how to tell and how much to tell.

In general, it is best to be as open as possible, even with quite young children. Remember, you yourself are likely to be affected by the news of any impending bereavement, and the child will sense that something is wrong. Because of the tendency of children to blame themselves, it is likely that the child will imagine that he/she has done something to upset you, if you do not explain.

APPROPRIATE TIMING

Appropriate timing for breaking the news of an impending bereavement will depend very much on the circumstances. Where the loved one is terminally ill, but is unlikely to die immediately, as in some forms of cancer, there will be time to take things slowly and gradually.

If, on the other hand, the sick person has had a series of heart attacks and may have a fatal attack shortly, then it may be important to break the news fairly quickly.

In cases of accident, particularly in traumatic circumstances, again, children benefit from being told as soon as possible. (See Chapter Five.)

WHO SHOULD GIVE THE CHILD THE NEWS?

It is best if a child is told traumatic news by an adult who is emotionally close to the child, with whom the child will feel free to express his/her immediate feelings and take personal support. The person who initially tells the child is more likely to be the person with whom the child will be able to initiate further talk and confide in at a later point.

BREAKING BAD NEWS

How you do this, and in particular how long you take to do this, is going to depend on many factors. There are general principles that are helpful to consider:

Time and Place
Because this is significant news that you are telling your child, it is important to make sure that you set aside sufficient time and are able to tell your child in a quiet and uninterrupted way. If necessary, take the telephone off the hook, do not answer the front door. If, for whatever reason, you are not at home, ask for a quiet place, privacy, and ask not to be disturbed.

Approaching the News Step by Step
Start by letting your child know that you have something important to talk about, and something that is sad. Check, if relevant, whether he/she has any idea what you want to talk about. He/she may have guessed a little of what it is likely to be. If not, then move further towards the topic by referring to the fact that, for instance, Uncle Fred has been rather tired or ill recently. Ask him/her if he/she has noticed this and give examples of times when you both noticed it. Then say that he has had to go to the doctor, who sent him to hospital, where, after tests, they seem to think that he is very ill indeed. Again, leave space for discussion, encourage him/her to talk about other people he/she has known who have been to hospital, and what it was like. At this stage, it can be an opportunity to point out that, in many cases, visits to hospital mean that there is an illness or condition that can be made better, but that sometimes, however hard doctors try, they cannot cure a person's illness. Again leave space to discuss this. Only then let him/her know that Uncle Fred is so ill that the doctors do not think that they

can cure his illness. Again, invite questions, allowing plenty of time.

You may, in the event of a sudden death, have to do all this in one sitting, but in a long illness you may have considerable time, and be able to have several talks moving through this process of preparation. As you tell the news, share your feelings with the child – whatever they may be: shock, bewilderment, helplessness, sadness, anger that this should happen – anything you may feel.

By doing this, you are helping the child learn that it is all right to express feelings. At the same time, the way in which you express your feelings needs to reflect the fact that it is a child you are speaking to. While it is appropriate to show your tears, or to say you feel angry, it could be overwhelming for a child to see you hysterical with grief, or screaming with rage.

Allow Time for the Child's Feelings
Ask the child how he/she is feeling, or just reflect on what you see of his/her feelings. If it seems right, and according to your relationship and the age of the child, hold his/her hand or cuddle him/her.

Repeat the Information
Take the time to go over what you are saying several times – be as concrete as possible. A child may be in a state of shock and not be able to take in what you say the first time. A younger child may need to hear you giving actual examples: 'Uncle Fred has died. He won't be able to come to Sunday lunch any more; he won't be able to do his crossword any more; he won't be able to

do anything any more.' As well as the concrete examples, use the words 'dead' or 'has died'. This avoids being ambiguous or confusing. You may otherwise confuse the child if you try to soften the blow by using euphemisms such as, 'We've lost Uncle Fred.'

Be Open
Be open and honest, giving information in a form that is understandable to the child. Again, use language that the child will understand, and say as much as you think he/she can take in at one time.

Give Space for the Child to ask Questions
Help the child to focus on any uncertainties about the death or the illness by saying that people always have questions when they hear about death, and he/she may have some now or later. Leave plenty of time for questions. Depending on the age of the child, and his/her experience, they may be quite concrete, or deep and wide-ranging.

Offer Future Opportunities for Questions
Questions about the nature of the illness may need to be repeated many times, and this can be hard if you yourself cannot grasp the details fully. If this is the case, just tell him/her what you know and then say that you don't really know the full answer either. Offer to find out, or to get a doctor or nurse to tell you both later. Also, tell him/her that if you find out additional information, you will pass it on.

Concerns about Responsibility

Be clear with the child that what has occurred is not his/her responsibility. However, you can also tell him/her that often everyone feels that it is a bit their fault when somebody they know dies. But, whatever has gone wrong, or whatever illness is involved, he/she, as a child, is not responsible. Even in cases of fatal accidents arising from play between children, it is the adult's responsibility to ensure that the play is safe.

Ongoing Support

Assure the bereaved child that the adults around him/her, (family and friends) will be looking after him/her. Tell the child not to worry about asking for extra time and attention, even if adults seem busy. You will then need to let others know that you have told the child this.

Who Else Knows?

Let the child know who else is privy to the information you have given him/her, and which other adults you will be telling. By doing this, you will enable the child to talk to other people concerned, and so widen the support available to him/her.

IF SOMEONE HAS A LONG-TERM ILLNESS

- Keep the flow of information and questions open between you – time needs to be made specifically for this, even if you are busy tending the sick person The child's needs are also important.

- Affirm often and in several ways that it is not the child's fault that his/her loved one is so ill.

- Explore with the child how he/she can be supportive to the sick person. It will make a difference to his/her grieving if he/she is included in the care. He/she may be able to take responsibility for refilling a water jug at certain times of day, or have a certain time which he/she spends with the sick person.

- Encourage the child to spend time talking to or about the dying person, reliving the happy and not-so-happy times and aspects of the relationship. Sometimes it can help to use old photographs as a basis for this.

- Remember that children have the facility to move in and out of their feelings of sadness more easily than adults – allow your child his/her other needs, to continue to play and to be his/her age.

- Keeping to certain aspects of routine will provide security for a child.

- Let other adults who have contact with your child know what is happening. Also, let them know how you are handling the situation and ask for their support for the child.

Chapter Five
SUPPORTING A GRIEVING CHILD

When a loved-one dies you may or may not have had time to prepare your child for the death and, however much preparation you have done, it is still likely to be a hard time for all of you.

WHEN THERE IS NO TIME TO PREPARE A CHILD FOR A BEREAVEMENT

In general, children benefit from being told about a bereavement as soon as possible. There are several reasons for this apart from the fact, mentioned earlier, that your child is likely to sense from your behaviour that something is wrong.

Where there is a traumatic accident, it is likely that there will be considerable activity among the adults, an exceptional number of telephone calls, visits to hospital and visitors. Children in the family need to know what is happening, to give them some immediate understanding of the changes. Even more important is that knowing the facts will prevent them from picking up small pieces of information and constructing an even more horrific imaginary scenario than that which exists.

If a child is not told the facts, but given a sanitised version and later hears the truth, he/she will lose some measure of trust in the adults. It can similarly increase the trauma if a child hears news of a fatal accident from a third source – such as the media. To avoid this possibility it is vital to pass on information quickly in these circumstances.

The principles of breaking bad news are the same as those outlined in Chapter Four. However, with a sudden death you are likely to have little time to prepare yourself, and will yourself be in a state of shock. You may, in this case, just need to take what time you can beforehand, to try to be clear about exactly what you will say, and be even more ready to spend extra time with the child afterwards.

WHEN THE DEATH IS IN SOME WAY UNMENTIONABLE

There are some categories of death that may be considered unmentionable either within or outside a family because of a stigma associated with the death or the relationship: suicide, death linked to AIDS/HIV, drugs-related death, or a death associated with a partner who has not been acceptable to a family. In these cases, the child's grief may be blocked because he/she is either not told what has happened and feels confused by the sense of the unspoken behind the half-truth, or in other cases the child may have nobody within the family who is willing to listen to his/her grief.

It is tempting to try to protect a child from these

'difficult' truths, but the reality is that, if you do not tell the child, he/she may hear them at some stage or another from somebody else. Not only may this be a shock and humiliation but, as with not telling the truth for other reasons, the child will not be able to trust you fully again.

On the other hand, young children are unlikely to understand complex adult relationships and behaviour. The task is to find the best way you can manage to tell as much of the truth in a way that a child can assimilate, and without telling a lie so that you can build on this truth as the child gets older. You may not feel it appropriate to tell a child that a relative has died of an AIDS/HIV-related illness, if you think that the child will tell others and be stigmatised at school. So you may focus on the fact that the relation died of, for instance, a very bad – and rare – case of pneumonia, and then, when the child is older, expand on this. In cases where an AIDS-related illness would not usually be life-threatening, make it clear to the child that this is very unusual, or that the person was very poorly anyway, otherwise the child may develop a fear that anyone else who catches flu or pneumonia might also die.

In cases where social stigma may be present, whether you feel it appropriate to tell other adults who may be able to offer additional support to your child about the cause of death is a matter for delicate individual judgement. It may help to ask yourself to compare the possible consequences for the child in the short, medium and long terms of passing on or not passing on the information. A teacher who knows that a child's relative has committed suicide may be in a better position both to modify any teaching content that may be upsetting, and to notice any particular teasing from other children, should this occur.

In any event, as children move through the different stages of development they do naturally 're-work' significant losses, and the truth can be expanded on gradually.

Children are often forgotten at a time of bereavement. They often hear and see things that give them a half-picture of what is happening, but they are also aware of the strength of the emotions in the adults and may not ask what is happening for a variety of reasons. Above all, they need to be given the truth, but in ways that they can understand.

Fred (aged seven), whose father had committed suicide, was told his father had died from flu, but somehow he knew there was more to it. He would construct any number of different versions of his father's death, very carefully watching adults' faces as he recounted his story, to see if he could get a clue from the listener's expression as to when he hit on the right solution. Initially, his mother was amused by this but, eventually, as the stories became more and more far-fetched and he began to be teased at school and excluded from friendships because he told so many different versions, she realised that she needed to tell him the truth.

It might have been better if Fred had been told from the start that his father had been very worried and unhappy, and that, although he had tried to be happy and lots of people had tried to help him, in the end he couldn't try any more. He was so unhappy that he decided to end his life.

In the case of an AIDS-related death, what parents decide to tell the child will vary even more than usual upon the age of the child. Because there is still some irrational fear about the transmission of the HIV virus, and in order to protect your child from prejudice and victimisation, it may be better in such cases to tell a younger child that the death was caused by another illness. With a teenager, who is more able to be discreet with the information, you may want to be completely open.

The effects on a grieving child of others with whom they come into contact is considerable – whether it is adults who understand and support, or adults who tell the child to, 'Cheer up, your mother will have another baby soon,'; whether it is other children who, because of their unease with death, either overwhelm the child with excessive sympathy, or pick on the bereavement as something to tease the grieving child about. In these circumstances, your support can make all the difference, and you can explain that others sometimes are unkind because they are frightened and don't know what to say or do.

SUPPORTING CHILDREN THROUGH PARTICULAR CHANGES

Parental Death and Secondary Losses

When a parent dies, there are often ensuing secondary losses such as loss of finance. This may lead to loss of home, and/or limitations on out-of-school activities.

There may be grants and other sources of income that can offer additional financial support. If not, these secondary losses also need to be addressed openly and the resultant feelings expressed.

Another form of secondary loss when a parent dies is caused by the redistribution of household chores. This may mean that there is less time as well as less money for the surviving parent to spend with each individual child. Just when the child needs additional support, the surviving parent may be very concerned with keeping the household going on a practical level, and be unaware that the child's emotional needs are in fact paramount. The cleaning will still be there next week – the child's unmet need for extra cuddles or time to talk could lead to grief becoming stuck.

Particular Support for Teenagers
Bereaved teenagers face special difficulties. They are likely to feel responsible for the surviving parent, and yet, prior to the bereavement, one of their developmental tasks would have been to work towards separating from parents. So, when a bereavement occurs at this time, a teenager will feel pulled in opposing directions. Teenagers can best be supported by ensuring that they do not take over too large a share of the parental roles. A teenager needs to be reminded that he/she is still only a teenager, and not an adult.

Exploring possibilities for teenagers to defer important exams for a year following a close bereavement, so as to allow time for the grieving without pressure, is another way of helping them cope.

Because teenagers are at a particularly vulnerable time in their development, they occasionally react to a bereavement by adopting risk-taking behaviour involving alcohol, drugs, sex, or even self-harm. Whatever the explanation for this, as a parent you should give your teenager as much support as possible; being there should he/she want to talk, asking other adults with whom he/she is in contact to offer their time to him/her, and explaining to his/her friends that he/she really needs their time too. Alongside this, you need to maintain expectations and boundaries consistent with those in place prior to the bereavement, to help him/her regain the stability he/she used to feel.

Hannah, whose dad died when she was sixteen and who became pregnant within two months of his death, explained years later, 'I only got pregnant because I needed so much to be really close to someone, and Mum was exhausted and angry with me. I just thought I'd take the chance.'

WHAT A GRIEVING CHILD NEEDS IMMEDIATELY FOLLOWING A BEREAVEMENT

Each child is an individual and will grieve in his/her own way, but, nevertheless, there are commonalities as to what a child is likely to need.

Physical contact and care:
- Cuddling
- Sitting close to you
- Extra warm blanket at night, hot-water bottle, extra jumper
- Warm drinks
- Light left on at night
- Comfort food
- Revert to family rituals associated with when child was younger
- Encouragement and opportunity to rest

Honest, caring communication:
- To be given information about the death
- Opportunities to talk about the bereaved person
- Opportunities to ask questions
- Opportunities to express feelings

- To be told that it is not his/her fault that the person has died
- To be told that he/she will continue to be taken care of
- To be reassured about the normality of grieving

- To be supported by continued routine where possible
- To participate in private and in public mourning
- Affirmation that it is fine to carry on with his/her life

- To be encouraged to choose a memento from among the dead person's possessions

SIGNIFICANCE OF TIME UP TO THE FUNERAL AND BURIAL/CREMATION

The Funeral and Other Rituals

During this time, while the adults tend to be preoccupied with practical arrangements, again children can be forgotten and inadvertently excluded. It can help a child if he/she is encouraged to participate in activities, such as having some say in the funeral arrangements – maybe choosing a poem, song or hymn as part of the service. A child may himself/herself wish to say a few words or read something. Children from infancy upwards can choose a flower or wreath. Some children may choose not to attend a funeral or burial, but it is important that it is the child's own choice. Many children who are not allowed to see the dead body or to attend a funeral of a close relative feel very resentful of this later in life. It can be of great help, as a way of making the death seem real, to visit and say a few words of goodbye to the dead person.

Preparing the Child for the Funeral

Of course, if a child does attend a funeral it is important that they know in advance what the funeral will be like. A child may never have been in a chapel or church before and will benefit from being told a little of what it may be like. It can help too if he/she is told what the format of the service will be, and who is likely to be there. Also, the child will need to know that he/she will have a particular adult to support him/her, to sit next to him/her and to be with him/her, keeping a watchful eye if the parents are likely to be unable to do so because of their own grief.

The public nature of a funeral, where friends and family are present to remember and mourn, will tend to lessen the feelings of isolation so common in bereaved children. If they are able to attend the funeral, they will have for ever the remembered sense of the others who came to mourn. In addition to this, there is something very primitive and deep-seated in the expression of rites of passage; at times when feelings are beyond words, somehow the coming together, the solemn and formalised enacting of a ceremony with words, music and flowers, and the subsequent gathering of those who attended the ceremony in a less formal setting, with some refreshment and sharing of memories of the dead person, helps to actualise the grief. It also helps to release the mourner, enabling him/her to move a step on from the initial disbelief.

Alternatives to Attending the Funeral

There are times when it is decided by the adults or by a child himself/herself that he/she will not attend the funeral. An alternative is for the child to be with a sympathetic adult and to plan and enact his/her own ritual goodbye with that adult. This may mean a special time of sitting and talking about the dead person, it may mean visiting a place that held special memories of the dead person, it may mean taking flowers somewhere, or planting a tree or bush in the garden, or sitting for a few moments with a favourite photograph of the dead person and reading a favourite poem.

THE EARLY MONTHS OF GRIEVING

Supportive Routines
During the early days, it can easily happen that all daily household routine is completely abandoned. It is important that it is re-established within a few weeks as a means of providing some sense of security for a child, who at such a time is likely to feel very insecure.

Simian (aged eleven), years after his grandmother's death, would refer again and again with bemused wonder to the fact that, for at least a month after his granny had died, he could go to bed whenever he chose.

Sharing Family Memories
Talking about the death and the dead person and expressing your feelings is best of all shared with the family, because it can act as a further family bond. In itself, it gives the child permission to talk, grieve and express whatever needs to be expressed in intimate surroundings. Photographs of the dead person, and any favourite and everyday objects linked to the dead person serve as good entry points. Within the family, favourite activities and shared memories will naturally lead to talk.

One aspect of talk that is helpful, although it feels quite brutal early on, is to use the words 'dead' and 'died', and to speak of the dead person in the past tense. This, too, helps the grieving child to move from denial of the death into an acceptance.

**Encouraging your Child to
Express his/her Feelings**

While talking about your thoughts, feelings and memories will be important in itself, it is also important that you are showing the child that it is all right to talk about what has happened, that it is not unmentionable, too devastating or complex to be discussed. Still more important will be that the child is given plenty of opportunity to talk and be listened to with the sort of attention that indicates that what the child has to say is worth listening to. Even if the feelings and thoughts that he/she is expressing are very different to those that you are experiencing yourself, it is important to let the child know they are valid.

The feelings involved in loss are so complex that the child will need time to accept and to sort out the confusion within, and as he/she does so he/she will get a clearer idea of what death actually means. This is best done, not by an adult telling a child what to think, but rather by continuing to listen, and reflecting back what the child seems to be saying, irrespective of whether you agree with it. If you tell the child what to think, you may get surface agreement and compliance, rather than giving the child a chance to really sort out for himself/herself what it is he/she thinks and feels. Of course, you will also let the child know what you think, pointing out, for instance, the factual differences between sleep and death. Do not deny or deride his/her fears. Listen to them and offer practical support – for instance, a nightlight or something else to make going to sleep feel safer.

'So you think that Granny is in a house in heaven

which is just like her one on earth?' would enable a child to go on and explore his/her ideas further, not necessarily at that moment, but later. But if you deny his/her own idea by dismissing it, or ridiculing it, he/she will be less likely to continue to bring his/her thoughts and feelings to you, and the grief work could then become stuck.

We all grieve differently. There are children who cannot, in the pain of their grief, talk easily of how they are, and with such children, just a regular physical presence, physical contact, extra cuddles and comfort food may be the best way forward. But talk to them about how you are feeling, and let them know all the time that you are available should he/she want to talk, but if he/she just wants to be quiet, that is all right also. It is important to support what is the right way for the individual child – insistence on him/her doing the grieving your way can in fact turn into a block.

Emotional Responses
There will be many and confusing emotions amongst a family. Accepting and allowing what is being expressed for each individual is helpful. Two responses in particular are sometimes difficult:

• Crying
Crying together can be especially supportive if each person is allowed to cry themselves out and stop in their own time. Loud sobbing and even wailing may be what some children (and adults) need to do. It is nothing to be afraid of.

• **Anger**

It is also good if the anger that is so often present is allowed and given a safe way of expression. Sometimes it can be made almost into a game, which nonetheless will allow for the anger to be expressed physically. Anger really released in this way will often lead to crying as one emotion passes into another.

Expressing anger:
- A good shout into your pillow, in the garden, out on a walk
- Stamping walks, imagining you're destroying something
- Throwing safe objects – foam balls, crumpled newspaper
- Writing rude words very large on newspaper
- Tearing paper, parts of old phone directories, old clothes
- Digging a deep hole/trench in the garden
- Hitting a pillow
- Wringing out an old wet towel
- Playing music loudly

Understand the Child's Need for Breaks in his/her Grief

Children's need to move in and out of their grief is often misunderstood both by adults and sometimes by the child himself/herself. It is often supportive to a child to have it explained to him/her that there may be times when he/she feels perfectly like he/she did before the death and may feel happy, and like engaging in all his/her old activities. By telling him/her this, you will enable him/her not to feel guilty about times when he/she feels as before. You will need to explain that it is not a question of a lack of love for the dead person.

Using Other Adults to Help

There may be times when the adults within the family find it impossible to talk to their grieving children because of their own grief. If this is the case, it is possible very often to find another adult who has some expertise and knowledge of the grieving process, and who can make themselves available to your child to listen and support him/her until you feel able to do so again. Such a person may be a health visitor, teacher, bereavement counsellor, practise nurse, social worker or priest. Your child will need to be willing to talk to someone else and, in some cases, may find it easier – that is, if the child himself/herself cannot bear to inflict his/her own grief on his/her parent who is also in mourning.

It will, in any case, help if other adults in contact with the child (such as teachers and club leaders) are told of the bereavement, because they will then understand any changes in his/her behaviour, and be able to make some allowances.

When inability to concentrate and unresolved feelings lead to disruptive behaviour, it is also worth keeping in good contact with the school, providing additional physical activities for the child (the ideas about releasing anger will help here), but also with the child and school developing some clear, supportive boundaries and limits, so that the child who is currently experiencing difficulty in containing his/her behaviour comes to feel that the adults around him/her really will help him/her to do this, rather than merely criticising him/her at this difficult time.

MOVING THROUGH THE GRIEVING PROCESS

As a child moves through the grieving process there may well be not just temporary changes in how he/she is, but permanent changes also.

Even quite young children may become suddenly mature for their age – this may show itself even without anyone telling the child, for instance, that now you have to help Mummy.

Joss was seven when his infant brother died. Joss had been a lively, high-spirited, sociable little boy, full of fun – he became much quieter and very solicitous towards his mother. He had never been told that he had to 'look after' her. His mother and father both had good support for themselves and did 'all the right things' as far as Joss was concerned. But the bereavement did undoubtedly change him permanently – he became a far more thoughtful and quiet child.

It is a matter of judgement to decide how much one should support by encouraging a child in an old direction, and how much one needs to accept the natural inner changes caused by a major bereavement, and be supportive of the new aspects that are emerging. However, one important guideline is that the child should be actively discouraged from becoming the protector or caretaker of a parent. This may mean the parent being very clear that he/she thinks it appropriate to get help and support from other adults, however much love there is between parent and child. It is the parents' role to protect the child, not the other way round.

Other Changes that can Occur

Other changes may be in the child's friendships, or in him/her wanting to give up activities. Support from the family, in finding a good way forward rather than pushing a child in an unwanted direction, requires a subtle knowledge of the individual. It also requires a sort of trust – trust that you as a family are doing what you can in the circumstances; and trust in the child and that what he/she is seeking to do is what he/she needs to do. It may be the right thing for a child to give up judo after his/her aunt's death. He/she may have been nearly ready to move on to a different interest in any case, and the bereavement has moved him/her into a more introspective direction. However, on the other hand, it may be that the death has led him/her to lose confidence and that giving up judo is a form of avoidance.

It is wise not to allow a teenager to make changes in what may be major life decisions regarding staying on at school, examinations or career choices at a time of bereavement. If in doubt, postpone, but encourage them not to radically alter their plans.

At times, bereavement can lead to behavioural changes of a disruptive, antisocial nature. The containment and channelling of this in a firmly loving way is called for.

Where such behaviour occurs, it is generally a signal that there is deep feeling seeking expression, and every opportunity should be sought to encourage and allow the child to express this in an acceptable manner.

The Importance of Memories

It can be especially helpful to a child to be told that they will never forget the person who has died, and that they may even want to find a way of keeping certain special memories fresh. A child can be encouraged to keep his/her own collection or album of photographs, or write a memory book of particularly treasured times. And, just as with adults, being able to keep some small memento can be especially healing.

Integrating the Loss

One way in which the sense of loss can be integrated with the child's present and future existence, is by recognising how the dead person has affected you. A child can be helped by having it acknowledged or acknowledging for himself/herself that his/her grandmother taught him/her to read, or that he/she has inherited his/her dead mother's red hair, or that the words his/her dead friend used to say before diving from the top board at the swimming pool, 'Go for it!' are the very words that he/she now uses to encourage himself/herself.

Chapter Six
YOUR OWN GRIEF AND ITS IMPACT ON YOUR CHILD

The way you are and the sort of relationship you have with your child will affect how your child is able to grieve. Also, your past bereavements and how you are coping with the present grief will impact on your child and affect his/her reactions.

RESPECTING DIFFERENCES BETWEEN YOU

Just as we are each different, so we grieve differently though we may follow some similar patterns. You may be a generally quiet and reflective person, while your child may be outgoing and physical. Your ways of expressing your grief will mostly arise from the sort of person you are, although you may behave temporarily out of character. How you are seen to grieve by others does not necessarily reflect how deeply you feel loss, nor the extent of your love for the dead person. Many people grieve in private while maintaining a calm public face – this is not the same at all as blocking the grief.

Frances was a very lively, active and sociable woman in her forties when her husband died suddenly. She was deeply shocked and turned away from the world. She gave up her part-time job and rejected her friends' offers of company. Frances needed to go over again and again what happened the day her husband died; she cried most days and, for months, every night. She slept fitfully and ate little.

Her son, James (aged sixteen) was of an academic nature, intellectual and with few close friends. He took charge of most of the funeral arrangements, and continued to support his mother, but also continued with his studies, and to socialise. While he wept in the period immediately following his father's death, within a month he had taken up his friendships and activities. He also began jogging regularly, as it helped him ease the tension he was experiencing.

The best support you can give your child is to enable him/her to meet his/her needs in the way that is best for him/her – and not to burden him/her with your expectations of how he/she will grieve.

Your Relationship with Your Child

There are some common ways of seeing yourself and behaving as a parent which colour much of your behaviour and set certain roles for you and your child. These may or may not change as a child grows and matures, but significant family events such as a close bereavement may highlight these roles, especially as they may pose particular challenges to the grieving.

Common roles that may interfere with grieving are those of 'the protector parent', 'the omnipotent parent' and 'the practical parent' – we all take on those roles as parents for part of the time, but if we over-identify with one role in particular we can make things harder for our child.

ASK YOURSELF ABOUT YOUR ROLE AS A PARENT

1. Do you discourage your child from taking risks?

2. When your child was small, did you think it important to complete all your housework before going to the park, even if it was a hot day and all your friends would be there?

3. Do you feel very guilty if you have forgotten to get your child's PE kit ironed for school one day?

4. Do you reassure your child often with phrases such as 'I'll make sure it's all right'?

5. Have you ever allowed your child to stay away from school because he/she was dreading a lesson?

6. Do you join with your child in blaming others when things go wrong for him/her?

7. Are you sure that your beliefs about education are the right ones, and are you critical of other people's beliefs?

8. If your child is hurt physically or emotionally, do you try to distract the child from the hurt?

9. Do you pride yourself that, whatever happens, you are able to cope with everyday life without letting upsets get in your way?

10. If your child came last in his first swimming race at the gala, would you encourage him/her strongly to still enter the next race?

11. Does your child take part as much in household chores as others of his/her age? (Check with their parents!)

12. Do you often tell your child that you know best?

13. Have you ever written an excuse note for homework not done, when your child has just forgotten to do it?

14. When you are angry with your child, do you stop if you see he/she is upset?

15. Do you automatically intervene with the school if your child is given a punishment?

16. Do you allow your child to see you depending on others?

17. If your child has broken up with a friend and is reluctant to go to school one day, would you insist he/she goes?

18. Is your child as independent outside the home as most of his/her friends?

(Answers on the last page.)

If you find from this quiz that you might be playing the role of protective parent, then the challenges for you in supporting your bereaved child will be:

- To allow and validate your child's grief

- To encourage your child to attend the funeral and share the public mourning
- To share some of your feelings regarding the bereavement with your child

If you tend to play the role of omnipotent parent, your particular challenges may be:

- Coping with your feelings of helplessness in the face of death
- Feeling unreasonably angry that the death has happened and blaming others – and recognising the reason for this anger (that you've been faced with something you cannot control)
- Admitting your helplessness to your child
- Allowing your child to explore his/her own ideas about death
- Asking for additional help and support from family, friends and professionals

Like many of us, you may tend to put yourself in the role of practical parent. Your challenges are likely to be:

- Allowing yourself time to grieve
- Allowing your child time to grieve

A Parent Experiencing Great Stress – the Overwhelmed Parent
At certain times in our lives, the demands on us may seem more than we can cope with: it may be money problems, relationship problems, housing problems, medical problems or the demands of being the parent

of a particular child. At such times, we may feel quite overwhelmed and only able to just about get by. We have no resources left for others.

The chances are, in many cases, that if your child is grieving for a close relative or friend, you may also be grieving, and your own pain may be overwhelming. This may make it hard for you to be fully aware of your child's grief, or you may even tend to discount it. Because our own grief can be of an overwhelming intensity, it is almost impossible to accept that others can be similarly devastated.

This reaction is especially likely to be towards children, because they are able to move out of expressing grief suddenly and move into normal childhood play. This is a temporary phenomenon and does not mean that the child will not suddenly move back into experiencing deep sadness. However, seeing a child happily playing with his/her peers makes it difficult to realise that he/she is still grieving, when your own adult grief may be still very intense and constant.

You may also be quite worn out by the need you have had to care for a dying loved-one, and by regular hospital visits, while at the same time keeping the family going. When the bereavement occurs you may be nearly exhausted and have little energy left for anyone else.

On the other hand, you may be in a state of shock following a sudden or traumatic death. This itself is a sign that the experience has been so overwhelming that, in order to protect yourself, your emotions have temporarily 'switched off'. Rather like after a bad case of flu, you may feel rather disengaged from life and feelings, and just be going through the absolutely essential motions in a robotic state.

And then, of course, you have the possibility of having been involved with the practicalities of the funeral, and making decisions about possessions and the disposal of the home of the dead person. Coping with these practicalities takes all the resources you have available. It is hard to find time for a child in all this, however much you would like to do so.

All in all, you yourself may be feeling very much in need of support, and feel quite angry that in these circumstances you should still be responsible for the needs of your child. 'Who is looking after me?' is the often heard cry of a parent in these situations.

If you are in this situation, it is important for you and for your child that you get access to whatever outside support is available to both of you. This may be practical help at the time of death, with funeral arrangements or with the necessary paperwork, or maybe in the months that follow, additional help with the housework. But also it may be that emotional support is needed. Friends, family and neighbours can be very generous with their time and help – but they often need to be asked, as they may not like to interfere. Or they may assume you are coping better than you are. Professional and voluntary help is most likely to be available through your schools, social services, GP and surgery, and the many voluntary organisations. (See Chapter Eight and Appendix A for lists of such agencies.)

Remember that, however you are feeling, you are

the parent and it is not your child or teenager's responsibility to take on a parental role in caring for you. There is a fine line between sharing your grief with your child and putting an unreasonable burden of grief on to him/her. Where too much is demanded of a child in this way, it can interfere with his/her own ability to grieve, and have long-term effects.

How Your Relationship with the Deceased Will Affect Your Own Grief

Death of Your Parent

If it is one of your parents who has died, you are likely to have the sense that you no longer have the support of one of the two people you have turned to for help all your life. In addition, you may begin to get a disquieting feeling of yourself as now being 'the older generation'.

However close children are to their grandparents, you may feel that they cannot possibly be grieving as you are grieving.

Death of a Partner

Here you will be faced with a daunting future as a single parent – with the new demands of running and maintaining family life single-handedly. It is also probable, if you are reading this book and have children in their teens or younger, that your partner may also be relatively young, and not of an age when death is normally expected. Such deaths are harder to accept. You, as the partner of the dead person, may well experience a certain amount of probably quite illogical self-blame: 'If only I had noticed that he was rather overweight. I should have made him eat more salad.'

You will also be facing the fact that you no longer have long-term intimate physical and emotional support, and the loss of expectation of what your relationship might have developed into over the years. There will be the deep sadness at the loss of the person you were sharing your life with.

All the plans that you had made and discussed with your partner will suddenly be impossible. The uncertainties regarding the future, and the family responsibilities which you will need to carry alone may be overwhelming at times.

Your child will also be grieving particularly deeply for their dead parent, and feeling all the insecurities which that implies. Difficulties may arise if you, through your own vulnerability, give the child the impression that he/she has to care for you – the child may then put his/her own grief on hold and in some senses become your 'parent'.

Where a partner has died, try to build in family support for the children. Your family unit has been weakened by the death of your partner. For your children in particular it is important that they get a sense of intimate family support and security. With only one surviving parent, the children will benefit from this wider support from relations. You may need to ask for such support because people are reluctant to interfere but, when asked, the family often are delighted to offer time and other resources.

Annie was five when her mother died. Both sides of the family stepped in to help her father keep the family together. One aunt came to stay for three months, other relations had the children for holidays, others regularly prepared meals and brought them round. Annie's awareness that there was family there for support has continued to be useful to her, especially in the upbringing of her own children.

Death of One of Your Children

This can be one of the heaviest losses to bear. There is often such a feeling of waste in the unrealised potential and also feelings of the lack of 'fairness' when a young life is cut short. Alongside this there is again self-blame. 'If only . . .'

Alongside this self-blame may come an increased anxiety about keeping the rest of the family safe. There may be a tendency to worry when the other child or children are not with the parent and, in extreme cases, the parents may not to allow the child the necessary freedom to engage in activities outside the home.

If the surviving child has been a close playmate of a sibling who has died, the loneliness of the survivor may be extreme. This is often made worse when parents turn to each other in grief and try to put on a 'brave face' in front of the rest of the family – it can result in a surviving child feeling excluded.

'They had each other, I had nobody,' said Thelma, years after her sister had died when they were both in their early teens.

When a young child dies, he/she is frequently idealised

91

by the family, and this too makes it particularly hard for a surviving child, who may feel that he/she can never be as good as the one who has died. He/she may find himself/herself constantly trying to achieve high standards in everything, almost in competition with the dead child. Alternatively, there may be a lot of anger if the surviving child has not himself/herself taken on board the idealised image of the deceased child.

'Sam wasn't always good – he was bad. He played out and wouldn't come in when Mum called,' said Stella (aged five).

The child is asking for you to confirm that her sibling was naughty, and that she can also be naughty sometimes. And for you to understand how angry she feels that everybody is speaking only of Sam's good points. You can support her by acknowledging his naughtiness.

Death of One of Your Child's Friends

While you may be moved and upset by the death of one of your child's friends, what more often happens is that, because you have not been so close to the dead child, you find it hard to acknowledge your child's grief. In the situation of 'best friends', your child may want to spend more time with the dead child's family, and they may welcome this. But it may raise a sense of discomfort and even jealousy in you – almost a fear that the other family are trying to replace their child with yours, and of your child feeling closer to them than to you as he/she is able to share their grief.

It may help you to acknowledge what you are

feeling, and perhaps then decide whether it is appropriate to share this feeling with your child. You should try to be as generous as possible in allowing your child to spend time with them or, if your child is older, acknowledging the time he/she may wish to spend with the other family.

HOW YOUR PAST MAY IMPINGE ON PRESENT GRIEVING

Past Griefs

Another aspect of your grief which can interfere with the normal progression of your child's grief is when a bereavement has triggered memories of past, unresolved griefs in a way that makes your grieving disproportionate.

Alice's whole family were grieving a dead pet. But her grief was particularly intense. Alice, who was in her forties, realised that she was actually grieving her dead infant sibling who had died when Alice was still a child. She needed to express this grief and explored it with a friend.

Unresolved grief is sometimes retriggered by a fresh bereavement, and the mourner needs to go back and work through that prior grief first, before mourning the current loss. This can be hard for a child to understand.

'Why is Mummy crying for Grandpa, when he died ages ago? Auntie Ethel only died last week,' said ten-year-old Sally.

Sally really needed to have it explained to her as simply as possible that her mother still had to cry a bit more for Grandpa, before she was ready to cry for her sister who had just died. It was not because she did not love her sister.

HOW YOUR GRIEF MAY AFFECT YOUR CHILD

If you are unaware of the normality and depth of some of the feelings you are experiencing, you may find yourself directing some of the feelings towards your children. You may express anger towards a child rather than towards fate. You may find that you express your fear and lack of security by telling your child that he/she will have to be your helper now. You may even tell a teenager that he/she is lucky, he/she has the rest of his/her life ahead of him/her, but yours is now ended. All these messages, and others, are ways which grieving parents inadvertently 'block' their children's grief because of the extent of their own pain.

By becoming more aware of what you are doing, you will have a greater choice over what you are doing. If you have done any of the above, you now need to let the child know that you have been inappropriate, and make a fresh start. This itself will help the child. Your fresh start could also mean finding the right level of adult support for yourself – someone to whom you can express your feelings and explore them further.

Of course, your past griefs may also have a quite different effect – that of preparing you to face the present or any ensuing griefs without feeling totally overwhelmed. For many people, the experience of having passed through a period of intense mourning does help with subsequent grief. Just the knowledge that you can feel this sad, this low and this angry, and that it can, in time and with the right support, pass, is itself supportive.

Taking Care of Yourself so that You Can Be of Best Support to Your Children

If you do not find a way of getting yourself as much support as you need, and also of caring for yourself, you will not be able to be the best support for your children. A useful metaphor is that we each have a 'cup of well-being' and that if we allow our cup to run dry, then we have no well-being available to pour into another person's cup. This taking care of yourself can be looked upon as having physical, emotional, social and spiritual components.

Physically
During the course of a bereavement, you may find your eating and sleeping patterns disrupted. Taking care of yourself in this area, therefore, involves making sure that you eat healthily and get adequate rest even if you cannot sleep.

If you find yourself either physically tense or very angry, you can release this tension and anger by taking plenty of physical exercise. Involving yourself in physically demanding household tasks – for instance, gardening or re-decorating – can be very therapeutic.

If, on the other hand, you feel exceptionally tired, allow yourself to take longer periods of rest and, if possible, during the first few months especially, ask for extra practical help from friends, so that you have some resources left to support your children.

Relaxation exercises can be very useful at this time – there are many tapes available which talk you through different ways of relaxing. For some people, the most effective may be through their breathing, for others, via music and visualisation, and for others, progressive relaxation, where you systematically tense and relax muscle groups throughout your body, or alternatively autogenic training, where you focus on inducing sensations of warmth and comfort gradually throughout your body. If one sort of exercise does not work for you, try another approach.

Socially and Emotionally
You may feel like seeing very few people during your time of grieving. But, again, it is not fair on your children if you develop a situation where they are your only social contact. Even if you prefer to see only a few people, or even just one friend regularly, it will help you not to depend exclusively on a child or children. Other people are often embarrassed around a grieving person. This is because they do not know what to say that you would find supportive. You may need to ask for what you want. Whether you want somebody to sit with you saying very little, or to have someone who will go for quiet walks with you, or somebody with whom you can just talk about everyday things. Try to let people know what brings you the most comfort.

It will help your child to know that you have other sources of support. It will help your child to grieve for himself/herself. As well as individual friends who may support you, there are a variety of organisations that may be able to offer either individual or group support.

Positive Things You can Do for Yourself

Share with Your Child and with Others
It is ideal if you can share some of your grief with your child, but, as stated above, other adults are also necessary. It is neither fair nor appropriate to share all your feelings with children, whether they are young children or teenagers.

Allow Yourself Space
Some people prefer to do the majority of their grieving alone. If you are one of these, be sure that you allow yourself the time for this. There is no rule that says everybody needs to express their feelings to someone else, but it does seem to be helpful to emotional well-being to express them somehow, somewhere. In this case, let your children know that you do your crying and your raging alone, but that you will support them in their grief if that is what they wish.

Other Ways to Express Your Grief
Your way of grieving may be through writing, painting or music. This may possibly be through contact with the artistic creations of others: many people find that

music, for instance, can either soothe them, or alternatively, bring the emotions right to the surface to be expressed through tears or words. Other people write, paint or compose to express their grief. Find out what is the best means for you.

In many areas, there are organisations which will provide counselling support for bereaved people. This can help if you do not feel you want to talk to anyone in your family or to any of your friends.

Spiritually
Whether or not you have a formal religious belief or affiliation, most of us have feelings, concerns or needs which relate to our deepest sense of who we are, and these can be called spiritual. At a time of mourning, some people will feel the need for additional support at this level.

• Receiving Spiritual Help from Others
Some of these spiritual needs are to do with the nature and purpose of our existence. Grief, leading as it does to questions of why this death has happened to this person or this family, highlights such concerns. You may choose to explore such concerns with the support of a transpersonal or existential counsellor whose training encompasses such issues. However, you may also choose to elicit support from a particular religious organisation or organisations, either in the form of individual support, attendance at services or exploration through reading.

• **Rituals as a Source of Healing**

Rituals of all sorts have long been recognised as having a profound and often healing effect, and have traditionally been used as part of all major rites of passage, including mourning.

For some people, rituals are associated with and are a part of their own religion or cultural tradition. But other people, with no particular religious affiliation, find solace through devising their own rituals – perhaps regularly lighting a candle and just sitting quietly, thinking of the dead person. Others use a particular time of day just to be silent and remember, or spend time each week in a 'special' place – perhaps by the grave. The regular replacement of flowers by a photograph in memory can be another soothing ritual.

• **The Solace of Beauty**

Another way of spiritual healing is being in contact with beauty – preferably in the open air. Time by the sea, in countryside or park, or sitting in a beautiful building, can be helpful.

HOW YOUR ATTITUDE TO THE FUTURE MAY AFFECT YOUR CHILD

Early in the grieving process, it may often seem impossible that life will ever hold any further joy. But, as they move through the grief process, most people discover a renewed pleasure in life. However difficult the loss has been, they can move on, taking with them some pleasure and learning from the past relationship, and having found out more about themselves through the grieving.

Do not limit yourself to living in the past – acknowledge it for what it is, for its pleasures and pains, and look to the future also. You are someone who has suffered a grievous loss – and you are more than that. This attitude will allow your child also to look forward and not to limit his/her life and expectations.

Chapter Seven
HOW YOUR FAMILY BELIEF SYSTEMS AND OTHER BELIEF SYSTEMS WILL IMPACT ON YOUR CHILD'S GRIEF

FAMILY BELIEF SYSTEMS IN GENERAL

A family belief system is the way in which a family knows and understands its world. Much of what happens both inside and outside the family is viewed through a particular mixture of traditions, assumptions, prejudices and expectations. Because members of the family are brought up to share these expectations, they act as a cohesive force, helping to sustain the family.

Belief systems such as 'In our family we talk to each other about all sorts of things', 'Feelings are important', and 'Children are important family members – not less a part of the family or less significant just because they are younger' will serve a family well at times of bereavement by encouraging children to share and express their feelings within the family. Some belief systems, and combinations of belief systems can, however, be unhelpful to children at times of bereavement.

We keep ourselves to ourselves

This is one belief system which prevents many families asking for help in times of trouble.

One child who suffered because of this was Robert (aged eleven), whose parents thought it unnecessary to tell the school of his aunt's death, as this was a private family matter and not to do with his education. It was not till the yearly report was published, when they found out he had been underperforming and his teachers described him as becoming rather lazy, that they decided to abandon their misplaced ideas about privacy.

If you tend to be a rather private family, you may want to consider altering this belief system in the case of bereavement, and to encourage your child to do so as well.

This may be a particularly hard decision when a bereavement is likely to be the subject of stigma. This might be the case when a sexual partner is not thought to be acceptable by the rest of a family, or when death is associated with drugs, alcohol, AIDS or a suicide. For a child who is bereaved by a death that is thought likely to be stigmatised by others, the burden of grief may be harder than usual.

Christine (aged thirteen), whose mother had committed suicide, was told that she had drowned, and only found out the truth herself months after the event because of a report in the local paper. Not only did she lose trust in the adults in her family who had deceived her, but also faced difficulties in her peer group who assumed that she had deceived them.

Children are too young to understand or to worry about these things

This is another family belief which can cause difficulties for a child who is bereaved. This is very often used when there is a miscarriage in a family. What often happens is that because the parents are grieving but trying to hide their sadness, the child may feel confused, sensing that something is not being said, and imagine that he/she has done something wrong. Alternatively, a child may understand in broad terms but be denied the chance to ask questions, or to grieve.

Sheila was ten when her mother miscarried, but she was just told that her mother had had to go to hospital for an operation. Sheila guessed what had happened, and felt sad because she had been looking forward to having a new baby in the house. She decided that she must have done something wrong because her mother was generally very protective and loving but now seemed to have little time for Sheila. It was not until her mother died that Sheila, as an adult, was able to express her own sadness at this loss of the sibling she was hoping for, and the fact that this loss perpetuated her position as an only child in the family.

Children very often know far more about what has been happening than parents realise, but they may only understand in part those bits of conversations they have overheard. So they can become very confused. Then again, they may hear of what happened from other sources later on and feel less trusting towards their parents. It can be far better to explain what has happened in simple terms so that the child can understand and share in the family grief.

We just get on with things – no point in dwelling on it
This is another belief system in certain families. This approach, stoic though it may seem, denies the family and all its members the opportunity to talk about and express their feelings, and to communally support each other in their grief. In fact, this attitude is more likely to cause conflict within a family, and to leave the family members feeling isolated from each other.

Death is morbid – we don't talk about it
This is a prevalent belief system in our society, even though it is not always made explicit. It is one of the reasons why we are so often unprepared to face a close bereavement. It results in a good deal of ignorance about the normal process of mourning, and it can leave children feeling very confused, curious and fearful about death. They may then feel trapped by conflicting emotions, and the more sensitive child may be quite unable to ask about what he/she would like to know.

IMPACT OF OTHER BELIEF SYSTEMS

Children in the family will nearly always experience a different set of belief systems outside the home, and will feel confused at not knowing which is right, and need to talk about this. If you are dogmatic about your beliefs, your child may feel unable to talk about his/her concerns with you.

Maybe a time of bereavement can be a time when

exceptions to these family belief systems can be explicitly made for the long-term benefit of the child.

CULTURAL, RELIGIOUS AND SPIRITUAL BELIEF SYSTEMS

Some of the biggest issues in family beliefs at times of bereavement are those relating to cultural, religious and spiritual beliefs. Because such beliefs are so important, often central, in upholding the family, they may be the harder ones to deal with when difficulties arise.

Some of the traditions surrounding death can be quite starkly conflicting. In some communities and cultures it is the tradition for the next of kin to participate in the laying out of the dead body, while in others this is the responsibility of professionals. Some religious groups keep traditions of wailing after a death, or of keeping vigil with the dead body until the burial. In other cases, the principal mourner will be visited by particular family members or friends with certain clothes being worn, and certain food eaten.

For many people presently living in Great Britain and Ireland, there is a paucity of observed traditions relating to death and mourning. Thus, in families where special observances are carried out, a child can feel awkward if unable to explain these rituals to his/her peers.

To support your child in a school situation you will need to let the school know which beliefs you have been instilling in your child. Also, you will need to explain to your child that many people may hold differing ideas to yours and his/hers so that it does not come as a shock when others contradict him/her. Teenagers find this easier to deal with, but younger children can be very hurt by other children's comments.

'Mum, you said Steve would be taken by angels, but Tom said he's being eaten by worms,' said Emma (aged seven).

The contradictions that your child faces outside the home may lead him/her to want to explore what the home beliefs really mean. So you can expect many questions to be asked, or at least that there will be many questions in the child's mind. Understanding this means that you can raise the issues that you imagine your child might be concerned with. Be ready to handle the confusion your child may be feeling.

Whatever the age of your child, but especially during the teenage years, it may be that the impact of the bereavement may result in your child no longer accepting your belief. Difficult though this may be, you may need to accept it and respect his/her views.

John (aged eighteen), rejected his previous Catholicism. 'Believe it if you want, Mum, I just don't any more,' he said angrily.

One way of dealing with this is to accept the rejection for what it is. However, it could be pointed out in similar cases that he/she is obviously very angry and that the strength of his/her feeling indicates how significantly Catholicism has affected him/her.

It may also be that your own views change. This may add to a child's confusion if he/she still is committed to your previously shared belief.

'We don't go to church any more, you always said we had to go!' said Robin (aged ten) to his mother after his dearly loved grandfather died. His mother could no longer bear to be in church because of her anger towards God, but Robin still wanted to go.

If this should happen to you, you could arrange for your child to attend church with another family, explaining to your child that you cannot manage it for the moment, and that you would feel it wrong to attend insincerely.

What Parents can Do to Help

• Encourage your child to talk about what is happening, opening up the topic of what other people outside the home may be saying in reference to the bereavement.
• Be ready to accept changes in yourself and in your child with regard to religious or spiritual matters. Let your child know that this may happen, but that it may or may not be a permanent change.
• Let the school know about the bereavement, and about the observances and beliefs of your family, so that as far as possible the school itself will not inadvertently confuse your child.
• Prepare your child to deal with differences in views or observances without feeling unduly threatened by them.

Chapter Eight
GETTING HELP AND SUPPORT FROM OTHERS

However good a parent you are, however much you may want to support your child at a time of bereavement or major loss or change, you may simply not have the practical or emotional resources to do so on your own. While much support is often available within a family, it can be even more helpful if you are able to share what is happening with others, and to use sources of support outside the family.

Support often comes from those who know what you have experienced and are aware and 'there' for you without making other demands at a difficult time. The simple presence of a neighbour who will come and be with you, perhaps saying nothing at all while you share a cup of tea, can lessen the feelings of isolation.

Other support may be of a practical nature – helping with the school run, or with the many pieces of paperwork that arise from a bereavement.

For six months after Henry's wife died her friends took it in terms to cook an evening meal for Henry and his two children, allowing him to spend time with the children after work.

Other people will be able to give you emotional

support – visiting, listening and allowing you to express whatever you need to. There is likely to be a similar support system available for your child.

SOURCES OF SUPPORT PRIOR TO AN EXPECTED BEREAVEMENT

When a bereavement arising from a long-term illness or condition is expected you may be able to ask for (and get) support before the actual death. This can be of great help, although you may nevertheless still need support after the death. There are individuals and organisations who are able to be of greater help at different times, and some may be able to help prior to the bereavement: your doctor's practice counsellor, local church, school counsellor, or hospice.

Support from the Medical Profession

Many hospitals and hospices offer great help to all the family prior to a bereavement. During the nursing of a terminal condition, there may be medical and nursing staff either in hospital or in the community who will help not only with all manner of practical caring issues, but also offer emotional support. A GP or other visiting professional may be very pleased to explain to a child in the family the nature of an illness, and what exactly is happening to the sick relative. Sometimes they may even have appropriate reading material to lend the child.

Anthony, whose wife was under the care of a hospice for the final months of her life, described the difference the art therapy made to five-year-old Tina. He said, 'She could talk about it all after she did her drawings – before she couldn't.'

Support from the School

At a time when there is serious sickness within a family it is always wise to inform your child's school as to what is happening. Again, not only will a school be able to make some allowances for changes in the child's behaviour, but a sympathetic teacher or tutor can be someone outside the family to whom the child may be willing to turn. They may provide emotional support at a time when the child may feel that the rest of the family is too preoccupied or too busy to go to for support.

Jane was seventeen when her mother died. She was able to see the school counsellor. All she wanted at that stage was to know that her reactions were normal – she had begun to think that she was going mad. Once she knew that what she was experiencing was normal, she decided that she did not want to continue with the counselling, but expressed deep gratitude for the one session where she could just seek information.

Because school is, for a child, very much 'his/her' own world rather than yours, you may want to discuss with him/her how, when and exactly what you will tell the school. Let the child have the opportunity to discuss and participate in the decision as to how far within the school the information should be passed on. This will be very much a decision dependant on the child's age and relationships with staff and other pupils.

Having discussed the situation with your child you may nevertheless make the final decision yourself – you are the adult in the situation who will have greater understanding of the long-term consequences of passing-on or with-holding information. If you have to go against the child's inclination, you will need to let the child know that you are doing so, explaining very carefully why this is so, and acknowledging your child's views and feelings.

Eight-year-old Susan was very upset to learn that her class teacher had told the class about the death of her baby brother on the day that Susan was at the funeral. Susan felt that she would have wanted to tell her class and felt she had been let down by her parents and her teacher.

In making such a decision, it is important to consider the consequences both of passing on the information, and of not passing it on. If the information becomes public knowledge through gossip and is not handled sensitively, it may not be helpful.

Theresa (aged nine) was teased when her peers found out from sources outside the school that her mother had died. This had a major impact on her – she began dreading going to school. The grief was compounded.

Support from Leaders of Out-of-school Activities
Similarly, the leaders of other groups your child attends such as Brownies, Scouts, sports clubs, youth groups, and church groups may all be able to offer support in an appropriate manner if they are told what

is happening. (See Appendices.) You will want to check which of these adult contacts have particular skills, knowledge or interest in supporting individual children within the groups they lead. Information about particular difficulties that a child is having to deal with is certainly something that most group leaders would welcome – even when they are not able to offer individual support. By being aware of the situation, they may be able to sensitively modify the activities of the group in order to allow your child to be as comfortable as possible.

Support from Voluntary and Self-help Agencies
There are many specialist voluntary and self-help agencies that support those with life-threatening or terminal conditions. Through joining such organisations (for instance Cancer Link or your local Muscular Dystrophy Association), you may well be able to access additional sources of support for your child, although most of the agencies or groups themselves work directly with adults. (See Appendix.) You should be able to find lists of such voluntary agencies through your local library, your local social services department, or through your GP or hospital.

'It was a real help to me when I went to the group,' said Sue, whose husband had been terminally ill. 'I got friendly with a couple of other mums locally. I felt I could cope then. They'd been through it when their husbands had cancer. They told me how to tell the children.'

It may be of considerable help to the child, both at this

time and later, to be made aware that there is a network of support beyond the family that can be called upon for help. The mere idea of a close relative or friend being near to death can be frightening and make the child feel very vulnerable. He/she may begin to consider who else may die, and who will then look after him/her. Becoming aware that there is a wide caring network in the community can be most supportive.

HELP FOLLOWING A BEREAVEMENT

Most of the sources of help which offer support prior to a bereavement will continue to offer you help after the bereavement.

Practical Support Immediately
Following a Bereavement

Immediately after a bereavement there may be many practical matters for the adults involved to deal with. It can be helpful for the child if you ask an adult outside the family to offer additional support. This may be as simple as asking the parents of a child's friend to have her for tea a couple of extra times during the weeks following the death. Or you may let it be known that you would appreciate another adult, who is close to the child, offering the child an opportunity to talk about things.

Obviously, the school will also wish to be notified, and would wish to be able to provide additional support. While adults normally receive letters of condolence after a close bereavement, it is not always realised how left out of this a child can feel. Many teachers will automatically write to a child and this is much appreciated. But if the school is not told, there is no chance for this.

Funeral directors can be very helpful in a variety of ways. Not only will they be happy to play a major role in organising the funeral, but they also will have suggestions about your child's participation, and many now have a special pack for children, including a simple booklet explaining the funeral procedures to the child.

Emotional Support

There are many local bereavement services that focus on offering counselling after bereavement, although they vary as to how soon after the bereavement they consider it useful to begin counselling. They may be able to offer individual, group or family counselling.

'No one else could let me talk,' said Sandra (aged fifteen). 'They were too upset, or just didn't want to know.'

Some of these agencies are part of a national organisation such as CRUSE. Many are affiliated to the National Association of Bereavement Services or the London Bereavement Network, and many others are run purely independently through churches, or at times in association with funeral directors. Again, your GP, hospital or social services should be able to provide you with this information. The British Association of Counselling will provide free information on request about professional counsellors in your area.

It may also be that a school has its own counselling service or a teacher trained in counselling skills who may be able to offer time to your child.

The counselling you may be offered from such services may take place either in your home or in a special venue with a quiet and private room available. The length of counselling that can be offered will also vary – some organisations only offer six to ten sessions, while others will offer longer term help. You may also need to check the experience or standard of qualifications of the counsellors.

You do not have to bear the weight of supporting a bereaved child alone. There are support systems 'out there' that will be pleased to help – and that have been set up specifically to do so. Being a good parent means doing what you can *and* finding appropriate additional help when you need it. It is quite surprising that few of us would hesitate to go for professional help to the doctor if a child suffered from a cut or graze that was not healing properly, yet we sometimes hesitate to ask for help for the same child's emotional pain.

APPENDIX A:
HELPFUL ORGANISATIONS TO CONTACT FOR SUPPORT

Practical Help

National Association of Funeral Directors,
618 Warwick Road, Solihul BN1 1AA   0121 711 1343
For names of local funeral directors

British Humanistic Society,
13 Prince of Wales Terrace, London, W8 5PG
Will be able to offer ideas as to non-religious funerals

Citizens Advice Bureau
Your local office (see local phone directory) will be able to offer advice as to finances

The Probate Office
Somerset House, London WC2   0990 143541
Will give you information regarding probate

Emotional Support

National Association of Bereavement Services
20 Norton Folgate, London E1 6BD   0171 247 1080
Can provide a list of local bereavement services

London Bereavement Network
356 Holloway Road, London N7 6PN   0171 700 8143
Can provide a list of bereavement services/counsellors in London. Most of these services offer individual counselling, some also offer groups

CRUSE
126 Sheen Road, Richmond, Surrey TW9 1UR 0181 940 4818
Can provide details of their branches

Child Death Helpline,
Great Ormond Street Hospital Freephone 0800 282986
This is a helpline for those who have experienced the death of a child of any age

The Compassionate Friends   0272 292778
*Organise local self-support for parents who have experienced
the death of a child*

Winston's Wish
Gloucestershire Royal Hospital,
Great Western Road, Gloucester GL 3NN   01452 394377
*Run week-nd camps for children who have been bereaved, with
parallel meetings for parents*

The Samaritans
*Local branches offer telephone support, and in some cases face to
face counselling. (See your local telephone book for number.)*

APPENDIX B:
FURTHER READING

Adults

Bereavement: Studies of Grief in Adult Life,
Colin Murray-Parkes (International University Press, 1972)

Attachment and Loss,
John Bowlby (Basic Books NY, 1980)

Living with Death and Dying,
Elisabeth Kubler-Ross (Souvenir Press, 1981)

Helping Children Cope with Separation and Loss,
Claudia Jewett (Batsford, 1984)

Beyond Grief,
Carol Staudacher (Souvenier Press, 1987)

Teenagers

How It Feels When a Parent Dies,
 Jill Kremetz (Knopf, NY, 1981)

Mama's Going to Buy You a Mockingbird,
Jean Little (Puffin, 1984)
Tiger Eyes,
Judy Blume (Macmillan, 1981)

When a Friend Dies,
Marilyn Gootman (Free Spirit Publishers, Minneapolis, 1994)

When People Die – A Book for Teenagers,
G & R Williams (Macdonald, 1983)

Books for Pre-teens and Younger Children

Badger's Parting Gifts,
S. Varley (Picture Lions, 1985)

Charlotte's Web,
 E.B. White (Harper and Rowe, 1952)

Emma Says Goodbye,
C. Nystrom (Lion, 1990)

Grandpa,
 John Burningham (Puffin, 1988)

Waterbugs and Dragonflies,
D. Stickney (Mowbrays, 1984)

When Uncle Bob Died,
Altheo (Dinosaur, Collins, 1982)

INDEX

ANSWERS TO QUIZ (CHAPTER 6)

Score 1 point under each heading as shown. If you score more than 3 in any one section, it may give an indication of a parenting role you have adopted.

Question	Protective	Omnipotent	Practical
1	YES	-	-
2	-	-	YES
3	-	YES	-
4	YES	YES	-
5	YES	-	-
6	YES	-	-
7	-	YES	-
8	YES	-	-
9	-	YES	YES
10	-	-	YES
11	-	-	YES
12	-	YES	-
13	YES	-	-
14	YES	-	-
15	YES	-	-
16	-	NO	-
17	-	-	YES
18	-	-	YES